# Good
# Butter
# Best

# Good
# Butter
# Best

**FROM DREAM TO REALITY**

Donny Willis

## LIFE**POINT**
P R E S S

Weldon Spring, Missouri

Good Butter Best: From Dream to Reality
A Publication of Life Point Press, Weldon Spring, MO, an imprint
of Pentecostal Publishing House, pentecostalpublishing.com

© 2021 by Donny Willis
goodbutterbest.com

Printed in the United States of America

Cover design by Timothy Burk

ISBN: 9780757761539

EPUB: 9780757761546

Library of Congress Control Number: 2020949603

*This book is dedicated to Ashley.*
*The one person who has*
*made me a better person every day.*
*I Love You More.*

# CONTENTS

## PART 1: DREAMERS

1.  Beyond Your Wildest Dream........................... 11
2.  The Roots of a Dream................................. 21
3.  Growth Cycle of a Dream ............................ 31
4.  Characteristics of a Dreamer........................ 47

## PART 2: GOOD!

5.  Good Thoughts....................................... 67
6.  Good Decisions...................................... 75
7.  Believe the Good ................................... 85
8.  Action—Get It Done ................................. 91
9.  When Reality Strikes................................105

## PART 3: A Butter TODAY

10. Little Things, Big Things .......................... 121
11. Embrace Big Moments.................................129
12. Butter on TODAY....................................145

## PART 4: THE BEST Tomorrow

13. Building upon Laid Foundations..................... 161
14. Hot Potato......................................... 177

Thank You ................................................ 187
Notes .................................................... 191

# Part 1

## DREAMERS

# Part 1

## DREAMERS

# BEYOND YOUR WILDEST DREAM

*"I have a dream." –Martin Luther King Jr.*[1]

People love traditions, recurring highlights in the year that peel off like the pages of a calendar. Your year may begin with a New Year's countdown, then continue through the months with red roses and chocolates on Valentine's Day, a commemoration on Memorial Day, a BBQ on July Fourth, a World Series in October, a Macy's Parade in November, and a family Christmas in December. We all have traditions.

A big tradition in my life is parades. In Louisiana, where I grew up, parades were embedded in our culture. No matter what town you lived in, you weren't far from a parade. There was the Mardi Gras parade in winter, the July Fourth parade, the fall Homecoming parade, and the end-of-year Christmas parade. Our church always had the biggest and best floats in the Christmas parade. While other groups had a regular cabbed truck pulling a trailer, our church's float was pulled by an 18-wheeler. The parade organizers always put our church at the front of the line!

When my kids were young, I took them to a local Homecoming parade. Spectators lining the route knew to bring a candy bag to catch the sweets thrown by the people on the floats. But my strategy was different; I brought a plastic basketball hoop with a laundry basket under it. The high schoolers in the parade couldn't resist the challenge to ring the basket, which produced the highest intake of candy on record. My kids were ecstatic! The people around us? Not so much.

Growing up, I never missed watching one particular parade—the world-stopping march down Sixth Avenue in New York City on Thanksgiving Day. I was mesmerized by the cheers, the band music, the elaborate costumes, and the colorful floats. I remember being in awe as the massive *Ronald McDonald* balloon passed by overhead. My favorite thing was to see Charlie Brown waving from the float along with his famed pet beagle, Snoopy.

Then the cameras would cut away to the big green square, and I can still feel my ears ringing with the upbeat tunes played by Broadway's latest and greatest. The parade would come to a climactic conclusion with the Singing Christmas Tree and the appearance of Jolly Ole' Saint Nicholas himself. That dazzling event marked the changing of the season—winter had officially begun.

## SCIENCE OR SHEER LUCK?

For me, the Thanksgiving parade was a sensual smorgasbord with larger-than-life sights, beautiful sounds, the taste of candy, and the contagious energy that made me want to be a part of it. Thinking of the colossal event puts me in mind of the common saying among my friends: "Go big or go home." That's how I feel about life. No doubt you've experienced that feeling too—and possibly the letdown that follows. Your incredible dream that looked so fantastic from afar changed when you woke up to brutal reality. The small flicker of hope that made you say, "If only . . ." eventually became "Not in this lifetime."

Why do so many of our audacious dreams become nothing more than daydreams? That's an interesting question, but I think it's more apropos to ask, "Can big dreams—big ideas—become reality? If so, is it science or sheer luck? Does the metamorphosis just happen, or can we make it happen?"

## DREAMS BEYOND SELF

Before we answer those questions, please allow me to introduce myself. I'm Donny Willis, and I'm a big dreamer. Throughout this book, I'll be sharing my dream and the dreams of those who have inspired me. My aim is to give you a road map to follow that will take you from dream to reality. But before we unfold that map, there's something about me that you need to know: I'm a history nerd, especially when it comes to the history of dreamers. So throughout this book you will read of people who dreamed so big that those dreams outlived them. Some of my favorites are Walt Disney, John F. Kennedy, Martin Luther King Jr., and the biblical character Joseph. These dreamers impacted their culture and shaped their world. They never saw the fruition of their dreams, so they derived no benefit from them. But that is the embodiment of a "dream beyond self." These people were able to look beyond their own imperfections, pains, and problems to see a world that did not exist and bring it into reality. They dreamed so big that the dream was more important than the dreamer. Like a rock splashing into still water, their dreams set off a ripple effect that altered generations. It may not have been on a grand scale at first, but the ripples kept widening until they changed the world. The effects of this type of dream are measured only after the dreamer exits this life. Later generations can then proclaim, "The dream lives on!"

All of us are products of a dreamer, the person who pitched a stone or a legacy into the pond of your life and set off a ripple effect. You may have derived great benefits from it, or you may have encountered unfortunate consequences. To you who have benefitted from your positive heritage, I hope this book helps you appreciate the blessings that came with it. To you who were hurt by the decisions of previous generations, I hope this book is a map that shows you how to change course and live a new life.

Let's look at some individuals who set off ripple effects that changed the course of humanity and are still impacting us today.

## WALT DISNEY

Walt Disney was a master storyteller. He was so good at it that he built one of the greatest empires the world has ever seen. But he didn't do it alone; his brother Roy, gifted with business acumen, kept the company on track. When asked about his success, Walt gave this answer: "I dream, I test my dreams against my beliefs, I dare to take risks, and I execute my vision to make those dreams come true."[2]

Outside of business success, his entire purpose was to bring joy and inspiration, and to push the scientific limits of discovery. He wanted to offer a world where people could forget their troubles and escape hard realities. Or, as Roy would say at the grand opening of Walt Disney World in Orlando, Florida, it is "a Magic

Kingdom where the young at heart of all ages can laugh and play and learn—together."[3]

## JOHN F. KENNEDY

Disney's dream was to bring people joy and inspiration, but John F. Kennedy's dream was to take humanity to the untouched frontier—more precisely, to put a man on the moon. Some claim his desire was simply to beat the Russians in the space race. Motives aside, one thing was undeniable: it was a big dream.

So, on May 25, 1961, President Kennedy called for a special joint session of the House and Senate with the goal of convincing them that an American needed to set foot on the lunar surface by the end of the decade. Once this dramatic speech was accepted, Kennedy took this dream to the American people. In September of the same year he stood on the football field of Rice University and declared:

> We choose to go to the moon. We choose to go to the moon in this decade and do the other things, not because they are easy, but because they are hard, because that goal will serve to organize and measure the best of our energies and skills, because that challenge is one that we are willing to accept, one we are unwilling to postpone, and one which we intend to win, and the others, too.[4]

His dream inspired a nation to believe in it and empowered thousands to make it happen. Kennedy never saw it because it didn't come to pass until six years after his tragic assassination. On July 20, 1969, Neil Armstrong stepped off the ladder of the Apollo space capsule, saying, "One small step for man—one giant leap for mankind."[5]

## MARTIN LUTHER KING JR.

Two years after President Kennedy delivered his "We choose to go to the moon" speech, another dreamer stepped forward. In 1963, Martin Luther King Jr. stood on the steps of the Lincoln Memorial and delivered a speech that historians labeled one of the greatest speeches of the twentieth century. His speech and mass march created a ripple effect throughout history.

As one who delivers sermons on a weekly basis, I find it interesting that twelve hours before the march was scheduled to begin, King was still so caught up in the logistics of the march that he spent no time preparing for his speech. I know the feeling. Some days have been so crammed with logistics that I don't remember I'm scheduled to preach until it's almost service time. When considering what remarks he would deliver, King chose the sermon title "Normalcy, Never Again." The speech highlighted American documents such as the Declaration of Independence, the Emancipation Proclamation, and the Constitution and how those affected the current culture.

The day came when they would march for jobs and freedom. After the march, it was time for King to speak. It seemed to be going well when a familiar voice called to him from the crowd. It was the famed gospel singer, Mahalia Jackson, yelling, "Dr. King, tell the crowd about your dream!" Without skipping a beat King veered off script, saying:

> I have a dream that my four little children will one day live in a nation where they will not be judged by the color of their skin but by the content of their character. I have a dream today . . . one day . . . little black boys and black girls will be able to join hands with little white boys and white girls as sisters and brothers. I have a dream today.[6]

The power behind that dream set off ripple effects that are still felt today. Recently, as I watched my three kids playing in a public park, I realized there was neither a "majority" nor a "minority" of any racial culture. The multicultural mix at the park was a beautiful thing. That moment transpired because someone chose to dream.

## JOSEPH

*"And Joseph dreamed a dream,*
> *and he told it his brethren:*
> *and they hated him yet the more."*
*(Genesis 37:5)*

Out of twelve boys in the family, Joseph was his father's favorite, and his brothers despised him for it. Then Joseph heaped coals on their hatred when he told his brothers his dream: the entire family, even their father and mother, would someday bow down to him. Up to that point, he was just a spoiled brat; now he was an arrogant braggart. They entertained thoughts of murder until one of the brothers came up with a more profitable way to get rid of him. They could sell him into slavery and make a dollar or two.

They threw Joseph into a pit until a buyer came along. Finally, after hours of listening to their brother cry out for help, a caravan of Ishmaelites passed by, and they sold him for twenty shekels of silver. Ironically, these people were from the "other side" of the family, the offspring of Ishmael, their grandfather's stepbrother. They had never seen eye to eye on things. The Ishmaelites sold Joseph as a slave in Egypt. Meanwhile, the brothers knew they couldn't tell their father the terrible thing they had done, so they killed a goat, dipped Joseph's colorful coat in the blood, and took it home to their father, saying, "Look what we found! Do you think this could be Joseph's coat?"

Although the coat was crusted with dried blood, Jacob recognized it immediately. It was the coat of many colors he had made for his son, similar to the overcoats worn by the nobility. In despair, Jacob began weeping uncontrollably because the evidence had convinced him that Joseph was dead.

The sad part about this story is that Jacob's conclusion was based on falsified "evidence." The brothers never actually told Jacob that Joseph was dead; they simply showed him the bloody coat and left it up to their father to decide what had happened.

The story of Joseph's life is similar to the journey of our dreams. *The coat may get bloody, but the dream is not dead!*

## BLOODY COATS

Walt Disney opened Disneyland in California in 1955 with the dream of bringing joy to families through wholesome entertainment. During the next decade he envisioned the "Florida Project," but his plans came to a halt in 1966 when he died of lung cancer. Roy refused to let his brother's dream die with the result that Walt Disney World opened its doors in 1971 with the Magic Kingdom, followed by Epcot in 1982, Hollywood Studios in 1989, and Disney's Animal Kingdom in 1998. Today millions flock to Disney World every year. *The coat may have gotten bloody, but the dream didn't die.*

In 1961, President Kennedy stood in Houston and declared his dream: "We Choose to go to the Moon!" That dream was fulfilled in 1969 when Neil Armstrong took that one giant leap for mankind. However, Kennedy never saw it. His life was ended by an assassin's bullet on the streets of Dallas in 1963, two years after casting the dream and six years before it came true. Yet today twelve men have explored the lunar surface. *The coat may have gotten bloody, but the dream didn't die.*

When Dr. King stood on the steps of the Lincoln Memorial in 1963, there was serious racial tension and hate. It was the opportune time to declare, "I have a dream!" In March of 1968, King participated in a mass march to support striking

African-American sanitation workers in Memphis. The march ended in violence. The next month he returned to Memphis to try once again and checked into his usual room at the Lorraine Motel. On Thursday, April 4, 1968, he stood with musician Ben Branch on the balcony of his second-floor room. It was almost 6:00 PM, when he said to Ben, "Be sure you play 'Take My Hand Precious Lord' at the meeting tonight. Play it real pretty." He was leaning on the balcony rail when a sniper's bullet ended his life. Although racial tension and hate have flared up throughout the generations since then, today the Willis children go to an ethnically diverse school. *The coat may have gotten bloody, but the dream didn't die.*

Even as Joseph's father, Jacob, was weeping uncontrollably while holding his beloved son's bloody coat, Joseph was far away in a foreign land being elevated according to God's plan. He went from being a prisoner in the pit to Prime Minister of Egypt where his brothers eventually came and bowed before him, fulfilling the dream. *The coat may have gotten bloody, but the dream didn't die.*

I don't know what dreams you have. Maybe after the initial euphoria they seemed to peter out. Maybe someone handed you a bloody coat and you thought your dream was dead. But I'm here to say, regardless of the evidence it's time to give your dream a second look. Hopefully, this book will bring clarity and definition to your dream.

At the beginning of this chapter I told you I was a dreamer. My dream is that whenever the last chapter of my life has been written it can be said of me that I fulfilled my calling and made everyone around me better . . . or butter. *Butter?* What in the world could that mean? Just keep reading. I promise you'll understand my "butter phrases" as we continue the story.

## THREE BIG IDEAS

1. Can big dreams—big ideas—become reality? If so, is it science or sheer luck? Does the transformation just happen, or can we make it happen?

2. A "dream beyond self" is defined by people who were able to look beyond their own imperfections, pains, and problems to see a nonexistent world brought into reality. They dreamed so big that the dream outlasted the dreamer.

3. Despite the evidence—a bloody coat—it's time to give those dreams a second look.

## THREE BIG QUESTIONS

1. What is your favorite tradition?

   _____

   _____


2. What dreamer(s) inspired you? Why?

   _____

   _____


3. What is your personal definition of the word *dream*?

   _____

   _____

# THE ROOTS
# OF A DREAM

*"You can do something in a manner
that no one else can." –Max Lucado*[1]

## DEFINITION BRINGS CLARITY

One of the traditions I enjoyed growing up was a yearly trip to
Baton Rouge. We usually made the two-and-a-half-hour drive on
a Saturday afternoon to get there in time to attend the Louisiana
State University Fighting Tigers football game. Being born in
Louisiana makes you an automatic Tigers fan. Even if you don't

like football, you're a Tiger by default. Something phenomenal happens on Saturday night sporting events at Tiger Stadium. Enormous energy is created by a hundred thousand pumped-up people pushing toward a common objective—to win! And when the clock winds down to 00:00, there's no question who won and who lost. Why? Because someone kept score.

In sports it's easy to determine who wins because the answer is posted in large, bold numbers on the scoreboard. But is it possible to keep score on dreams? Can a person keep score on life? If the answer is no, how can anyone determine who won? These questions are important because uncertainty breeds confusion, and definition brings clarity. The path to success becomes clear only when you pinpoint what you want. I'm going to help you do that by asking the following questions: Who are you? Why are you here? What do you want? Everyone wants something. The key to success is formulating a clear definition of what you want.

## WHO ARE YOU?

This is not a pie-in-the-sky book alleging you can do or be anything you desire. You've heard it before—be a butcher, a baker, or candlestick maker. Be a president, a concert musician, or a basketball player. All you have to do is work hard enough. But can you? Can an acorn become a rose? Can a sow's ear become a silk purse? Can a klutz become a graceful ballerina? I don't think so. But can you fulfill your God-given purpose? Yes! Absolutely. You are uniquely designed to accomplish what you were destined to do. Consider this assertion from a purely scientific frame of mind. Each of us has a unique set of genes. It's impossible for anyone else, in the past or in the future, to possess that same DNA code. The only exception is if you're an identical twin. However, there is more to our genetics than just that. According to the University of Miami Miller School of Medicine, "During development in the womb and after birth, our surroundings, exposures, and nutrition influence how our genes are expressed and how our bodies and minds develop." In other words, scan history and you will find that there are no duplicates or replicas of your life, for we are, as the apostle Paul described, "God's workmanship."

Let's settle this right now. You can't be your hero dad or your favorite singer. You can't be your congressman or your college professor or the doctor who helped you win the fight against cancer. You can imitate the actions and strategies of people you admire, but you can't *be* them. You can only be you. If God had wanted you to be them, He would have made you them. There are no duplicates; you and your ideas are "you-nique."

## WHY ARE YOU HERE?

It has been said that the two most important days in a person's life are the day of birth and the day of purpose. In other words, the day you were born and the day you figured out *why* you were born. This sobering reality forces you to dig deeper into the recesses of your mind and your desires by asking even harder questions, because the answers to those questions will define your purpose.

In the year 1543, the vantage point of the world was shaken to its core. Up until then, everyone thought of themselves as the center of the cosmos. Everything revolved around their views and their livelihood. Then along came a Polish man with a bony nose and thick accent carrying his maps and drawings. His name was Nicholas Copernicus. With one hand he tapped humanity on the shoulder; with his other hand he pointed toward the sun and said, "Behold the center of the solar system!" This proclamation, that the earth rotates around the sun, shifted the view of humanity. In the same sense, we as individuals must come to the realization that there are more views than our self-centered ones. This realization should cause us to begin asking questions.

I remember sitting in a classroom my freshman year of college when the instructor entered and asked the class a simple yet loaded question: "Why are you here?" Then, after a long pause for dramatic effect, he began his lecture. He wasn't asking why we were taking that particular course; his question probed much deeper. At first the question seemed pointless, but it proved to be one that challenged our thinking.

Now I'm asking you: "Why are you here?" Or if I could rephrase and ask, "What is your dream?"

What are you really looking for? What lifts you to a new level? What makes you want to get out of bed on a winter's day, grab hold of the day, and make the most of every moment? What gives meaning to your life? What enables you to navigate the confusion of a world that changes with every nanosecond?

## WHAT DO YOU WANT?

I have a three-year-old named Claire. Her Pre-K teacher said to us, "Claire, has above average determination." That was a nice way of saying she is hardheaded. But to her credit, Claire knows what she wants. The other night we were all at the table eating dinner—except for Claire. There was an eerie quiet. Quietness at our house is a rarity. So without saying anything, I got up to go look for her and found her in the bathroom rummaging through the cabinet with the child safety lock on it. You see, Claire has an obsession with Band-Aids. Her baby dolls all have booboos that need to be fixed. So we've learned we have to hide the Band-Aids, a job we apparently didn't do because she found them. She knew what she wanted and didn't stop searching till she found them.

When Claire saw me, she locked her eyes on mine and said, "Daddy, I almost have them, but I can't reach them. Can you help me?" I'm not sure if this was nature or nurture, but she went beyond her natural ability to get what she wanted, and after she had gone as far as she could go, she asked for help. I opened the door and pulled out the Band-Aids. If she was going to go through the trouble to search, find, and ask, I was going to help her finish the job. (She may also have me wrapped around her little finger.) She knew what she wanted and went beyond her limitations to get it.

We are designed to push the limits and move forward. What do you want? Are you willing to go beyond your limitations? I believe there is an inborn drive within all of us to go beyond our limits and reach for the desired goal. Without that desire, our lives are only a shadow of what could be. Admittedly, life can be lived without pursuing dreams. You can function without passion. But where is the excitement in that? Life is not a spectator sport. Get in the game! Clarify what you want and go for it! Do you want significance? To create a better world? Be a better person or spouse? Something materialistic or career related? No matter what your ethnicity, gender, or age is, it doesn't matter. Everyone wants, but how do you define what you want?

I hope this book will unveil that magnificent purpose. But a word of caution: the world will never accept your purpose until you accept it and believe it's worth sharing. If you believe the dream is worth sharing, then you will more than likely have the confidence to communicate it in such a way that it connects. Social psychologist Amy Cuddy wrote a book about what she calls "presence." She said, "Presence stems from believing in and trusting yourself— your real, honest feelings, values and abilities. That's important, because if you don't trust yourself, how can others trust you?"[2]

Understanding your own presence and being aware of how you present yourself motivates you to leave your comfort zone and share your purpose with the world. Knowing who you are, why you are here, and what you want matters. When you trust yourself and are a good steward of your dream, others will trust in your dream too. That's when things can really take off. Please allow me to tell you about the unique dreams that shaped my life. I hope my story inspires you to dream as well.

## THE ROOT OF THE DREAM

First let me say that all dreams have roots. What you desire has a genesis; it begins with you or with your past. You already know I enjoy history, but something even more fascinating is research-ing my own family history, which, I must admit, is filled with the good, the bad, and the ugly. I don't discredit any of it because I can't change the past, but those family roots are there, so I may as well embrace them as my own and learn from them. Some of the stories I've dug up about past family members have made me want to crawl in a hole and disappear. Others I'd like to repot and set them in a prominent place to enjoy and contemplate how these roots affected me personally. How did I arrive at the place where I pastor in New York with the purpose of planting churches? That passion didn't develop overnight. Curiously, I found it was actu-ally generational. I'll start with Albert and Arizona.

## ALBERT AND ARIZONA

It was January 2017, and I was sitting in my church office prepar-ing a set of interviews that our pastor was going to use in a new preaching series titled "This Is My Story." I looked up to see my great uncle walk through the door, ready for his interview on the history of the church. But I could tell there was something else on his mind, I guess because of the papers he held in his hand.

As always, he grabbed a cup of coffee before walking over to my desk. He handed me three pages of notes written by his sister, my great-aunt. As I riffled through the pages, he began telling me these were stories about my great-grandparents. These stories were meticulous, including dates, locations, prayers answered, miracles that happened, and a whole lot of faith.

You've never heard of Albert and Arizona Jackson, but they were my great-grandparents. The only picture I've ever seen of my great-grandfather is in a painting that hangs in my grand-parents' home. He's sitting astride his horse. Albert and Arizona helped plant three or four churches in Southwest Louisiana. In March 1988, a few days before her eightieth birthday, Arizona was sitting in her rocker, staring out the window. She began to talk. Her daughter quickly picked up a pen and some paper and began transcribing her words:

> It was around 1915 when we went to an old storefront building on the corner of Green Road. As Johnny Williams preached, the people were outside throwing rotten tomatoes at them. A few years went by and Mom heard there was a camp meeting over in Goss Port near the railroad. It was summertime, and I felt the urge to go to the altar. I was the first one out of a family of nine kids to receive the Holy Spirit, and we were baptized in Jesus' name in the Calcasieu River near the railroad tracks.
>
> A few years later, in 1926, I married Albert. He wasn't crazy about my love for church and told me that if I didn't quit attending, he would slash my tires and then walk off and leave me. I just kept singing specials and teaching Sunday school. My faith never wavered.
>
> We had a large family of ten. I didn't beg Albert to go to church. On the few occasions I asked him, the answer was always no. But it changed one day when he was coming home from East Texas and his car caught fire and he almost didn't escape. That's when he promised God he would find an altar of repentance. He borrowed a car that night and came home blowing the horn. He ran into the house screaming, "Get ready! I've got to find a church!" We drove to Port Arthur that night and went to church. Nothing is impossible with God.
>
> In 1932, at a camp meeting in DeQuincy, Louisiana, our third child became violently ill. I never

once thought of taking him to the doctor or the hospital. My only hope was prayer. I brought him to the altar and the ministers prayed for him. He had no pulse or heartbeat, so they took him outside. Then "old Bro. Bennett got in touch with the Healer" and all of a sudden, my boy began to breathe and was healed. We rejoiced and went back to the tent praising God!

In the late 1940s, Joe Duke came to preach and stayed at our home. One night we took him to Pitkin. We loaded up the tent in the car, and Albert loaded up our old upright piano on the back of his pickup truck and brought it to the tent so there could be worship.

Arizona paused and said, "Well, Albert has gone on to his reward. Three children and one grandson have passed from this life. God is my refuge and strength." And then the familiar words that can still be heard rolled off her lips: "There is nothing impossible with God!"

## A FEW MORE STORIES

I recently made two phone calls, one to my grandfather and the other to my great uncle. I asked them to tell me the story of the role my great-grandfather played in planting the church I grew up in. They told me of a time when people were extremely poor, and America was just coming out of the Great Depression. The people in Moss Bluff could not afford to drive to Lake Charles to go to church, so they began holding a tent revival with a preacher by the name of Joe Duke. That revival was so successful that they bought two pieces of property to start two churches. One property was on English Bayou, and the other was on Long Road off of You Winn Road.

My great-grandfather had some good friends in South Lake Charles who were house movers and owned some timberland.

Timber didn't cost much at that time, so he was told to cut as much timber as needed for the two churches. They started cutting down the trees and hauling them to the sawmill, using a borrowed team of mules. After the lumber was dry, the men began building the first church in Moss Bluff, then went to the other side of the river on English Bayou and started building a second church. My grandpa said he remembers when the church was built that my great grandmother stood up and testified, "I thank God for giving us a church this close to home."

Both men recalled that when this church was without a pastor, my great-grandfather would serve as interim minister. His decision to help plant a church was not based on emotion or their history, but rather on their vision for the future. Those beginnings were the roots of that church in South Louisiana. All dreams have roots. Even though I never met my great-grandfather, the impact of his decisions left a major ripple effect on my life, because one of those churches he helped plant was the one where I grew up, and where I received my passion for church-planting. Today, I pastor a church in New York and desire to follow Great-Grandpa's lead by leaving a ripple effect for the generations that will follow me. We do not build for ourselves but for those who come after us.

## THREE BIG IDEAS

1. How do you keep score on dreams? How do you keep score on life? How do you define what you want? These questions are important because definition brings clarity. The path to success becomes clear as you pinpoint what you want.

2. Your desire has a genesis. All dreams are born somewhere; they are rooted in your past.

3. Your dreams have a past, but they don't keep you there; they build you for the future. You aren't building for yourself but for those who will come after you.

## THREE BIG QUESTIONS

1. Who are you?

   _____

   _____

2. Why are you here?

   _____

   _____

3. What do you want?

   _____

   _____

# GROWTH CYCLE
# OF A DREAM

*"Dreams come a size too big so we
can grow into them." –Josie Bisset[1]*

I've kept a journal since 2004, and, as you can guess, it has helped
me write this book. There's something special about the opportunity to read life in retrospect. It has brought new perspective
and questions about past decisions and helped me make better
ones. I recently came across an interesting journal entry from
2008, but before I share it with you, please indulge me to place
the circumstance within personal context.

I grew up in Louisiana and went to college in Texas. My first full-time job after college was back in Louisiana. Before moving to New York in 2017, I had never lived over five hours from my hometown. Following undergrad studies, Ashley and I were student pastors in Wisner and Thibodaux, Louisiana. We then served as assistant pastors in Moss Bluff, and then as Lead Pastor in New York. With that in mind, check out this letter I wrote to myself in January 2008:

> It is now 2018 and I, Donny Willis, am happy living with my wife and child in the booming, never-sleeping city of New York. It's been a trying ten years since I left Texas Bible College. However, God has continued to bless my family, and I, with resources and "tough skin," intend to stick it out and grow a church. We continue to progress into the future with great hope and aspirations. This letter is nothing more than a simple progress report of the last ten years.
>
> Let's see how close I was . . .
> - ✓ Happily married
> - ✓ Have one child by 2018 (In 2018 we had our third.)
> - ✓ Living in New York
> - ✓ Enjoying God's blessing

Things have turned out to be even more memorable than I predicted. But here's what I like: I clarified my dream in 2008. You may be wondering what possessed a small-town Louisiana boy to dream of living in the New York City Metroplex. I've asked myself that big question many times. Hopefully, my answer will help you shape your dreams.

## WISNER

Our dream was to plant a church in the New York City Metroplex. We had harbored that dream, like a massive ship dry-docked in the port of our mind, for nearly a decade. The dream was conceived during my college days, but it didn't happen right away. Fresh out of college, I had only one opportunity: move to the small town of Wisner, Louisiana, population 900, give or take a few. That's a far cry from New York City. I told my first boss in Wisner, "One day I'm going to pastor in New York." I wanted him to know just in case the door opened, I intended to walk through it. But with that said, I didn't live in a New York state of mind; I lived in a Wisner state of mind. I don't believe you can succeed in one place if your mind is in another. Your dream won't be fulfilled if you frown upon present opportunities. I was young; the town was old. But some of the greatest life lessons I ever learned came from that small town.

I can still see myself sitting on the outdoor swing at the Gallops' home listening to old stories. Every story had a point; one in particular was about the value of faith. I still recall one of the first conversations with my new boss, the pastor who had hired me to oversee the youth ministry of the church. Attempting to do my due diligence and learn of the town's school culture, I asked how large Wisner High School was. He replied, "Oh, that school was shut down and consolidated years ago. But high-school-age students still live in town." Further questioning brought to light that in the summer the young people loved to hang out at the snow cone stand. So I hung out at the snow cone stand too, inviting students to the "new youth group" in town—although it existed only in my head. I lived across the street from the church, so on Wednesday nights I began a youth group hangout. I would take the couch out of my living room and move it to the church. I went to the local store and purchased cokes and ice-cream. The plan began to work.

Over time, the youth group's reputation grew. We had created "the coolest place in town." Honestly, in a town of less than a thousand, that wasn't difficult to do. We turned the second largest room in the church into a youth room and filled it with colored lights, rocking music, Xbox games, and a snack bar. Ashley and I would pick up between five to ten students weekly, and in two years, with the help of the Wednesday night "Summit," weekend "parties," and a lot of pizza, our small-town youth group grew from eight students to over fifty. We baptized over fifteen students, and the group kept growing at a rapid pace. We were the talk of the town, Facebook was blowing up, and the season was special. To this day I'm still closely connected to the people of Wisner. They taught me how to love, listen, and enjoy the slow life.

## THIBODAUX

An opportunity opened up to become the student pastor at the House of Prayer in Thibodaux, Louisiana. That church was larger than the town of Wisner, so it was a culture shock. One of my first conversations with the pastor included my usual disclaimer: "God called me to New York, so if the door opens, I'm going to walk through it." But once again, I didn't live in a New York state of mind; I lived in a Thibodaux state of mind, immersing myself in the Cajun culture. One of the first church services we attended was on a Friday night. All the songs were Cajun style with washboards and harmonicas. It was great. We were loving the fact that we lived on the outskirts of New Orleans, which meant Café Du Monde and crawfish season!

Thibodaux was a personal yet professional working environment, which means the church had staff meetings. Up to this point, I had never sat in a staff meeting. For the previous two years of my life the strategy had been simple: I'd have an idea, and we did it. Now I was going to weekly staff meetings, talking things through with a team, and listening to their input. It was a whole new world. But that was a good thing. I learned to listen to those around me because the best information helps makes the best decisions.

## MOSS BLUFF

My last stop before New York was my hometown of Moss Bluff. This church is full of people I deeply love, people who saw me grow up. Some people enter the stage of your life for specific seasons; other people, if they outlive you, will be at your funeral. The Moss Bluff church family was that kind of people. The place reminded me of my roots and gave me confidence for the future.

Moss Bluff is a missions-minded church that sends. Churches should not be hoarders of people; they should be senders of people. Moss Bluff has sent men and women all over the United States, preaching and teaching the kingdom of God. I'm so thankful for their vision, "Go ye means go me!"

## NEW YORK

For ten years that ship had been dry-docked in the harbor, and it was high to launch—either that, or retire the dream. So we made the decision to move forward with the dream, and in October 2016 we began what we thought would be a very long process. We applied for a missions program that would help us raise a five-year budget over the course of two years. We planned to begin the fundraising program in September 2017 and projected to be done by September 2019. Then we received the call that interrupted our plan, overturned our lives, and forced us to make new decisions.

## THE GROWTH CYCLE OF A DREAM

Do dreams automatically come true? The answer is no. I believe it is a process. The bigger the dream, the greater attention must be paid to the process. Good intentions are never enough. There must be a systematic process and a clear picture inside of your head that compels you to move forward. As one man said, "Everyone ends up somewhere in life. A few people end up there on purpose."[2] There must be direction and guidance for any dream to take wings.

Take a trip down memory lane back to *The Magic School Bus*. Do you remember the episode about the water cycle? Water Cycle = Collection → Evaporation → Condensation → Precipitation. Dreams have a similar growth cycle. I debated on calling it the lifecycle of the dream, but the trajectories of great dreams soar beyond a person's life span; they are so great they never stop growing. The growth cycle of a dream is the following:

I believe the process from a thought to reality lies in this simple definition: When an idea of what *can be* turns into a compulsion of what *must be*, you have birthed a dream, which then becomes your reality. As we briefly overview each item, it's important to think "steps" and not "programs." Thinking in terms of the next step means you are intentionally moving in a systematic process toward a known end. So the first question would be, "What is the dream?" and the second question would be, "How do I get there?"

## THOUGHTS → DECISIONS

It was Sunday, February 5, 2017. We were sitting at a table in Popeye's Louisiana Kitchen with some good friends when I received a text from a pastor in New York. He was the founder of Westchester Church in Valhalla, New York, located approximately twenty miles north of Times Square. His text simply read, "Call me when you can." I slid my phone over to Ashley and said, "I wonder what this is about." She shrugged, and we turned our attention back to our fried chicken. The lunch ended, and as I was driving home alone in my truck, I called the pastor. After a few pleasantries, he began to tell me that he was resigning the pastorate of Westchester Church. Remembering from previous conversations that I had a passion for New York, he asked if I was interested and if I could be there in twenty-one days (which would be February 26, 2017) to meet the church family.

I thanked him for the high honor and requested time to discuss with Ashley, pray about it, and I would give him an answer by Wednesday of that week. Pulling into our driveway, I climbed out of the truck, took a deep breath, and walked into the house. As I walked in Ashley immediately said, "Our timeline is moving up, isn't it." I nodded and began to relay my phone conversation. In an attempt to ease any concern, I told her, "I asked for a few days to pray about it." She responded, "You've been praying about it for ten years!"

Three hours later I returned the pastor's call and accepted his invitation to come. That night we booked tickets for our family to New York City. We would fly into LaGuardia on February 24, 2017, and fly back home on March 1.

Much like the past three years of living in New York, the events that transpired over those days were beyond belief. One of the events started with a simple Facebook post. Nathan, a recent graduate from the University of Florida posted that he was moving to Westchester County, New York, and was looking for a church. A friend of mine saw the post and knew we were thinking about moving to Westchester to pastor a church and tagged me in the post. We connected, and the young man ended up moving to New York the same weekend we did. Within the next few years, Nathan became the assistant pastor of Westchester Church. This is just one of the stories that helped move the dream from a thought to reality.

The next step in the process was that we agreed to allow the current members of Westchester Church to vote on electing us as their pastor. The vote would take place on March 7, 2017, only seven days from our departing flight out of LaGuardia. It was the longest seven days of our lives. Seven days to wonder if they would elect us. Seven days to ask ourselves, "What were we thinking?!" Seven days to wonder whether we should be gearing up for the big move or forgetting the whole thing.

In Moss Bluff we had a dream home with low property taxes. We were financially secure; we both had good jobs. We were surrounded by people who loved us. To top it all off, we had nearby family members. (Can you say "instant babysitters"?) All of those wonderful things caused our thoughts to drift from the sunny side toward the dark side. Because dreams often carry a cargo of fear, worry, and anxiety. There is no greater fear than that of the unknown.

Now, all of a sudden, we were having discussions about leaving it all to move 1,300 miles into a new reality with unfamiliar surroundings, no home, no financial security, to rub elbows with people we didn't know. To top it all off, no family. (Can you say "no babysitters"?) What were we thinking?

The seven-day silence dragged on and the call seemed to never come. March 7 was crammed with distractions, and I was operating on less than two hours of sleep. Finally, the call came: "Pastor Willis, Westchester Church has unanimously elected you pastor. Do you accept?"

## DECISION → BELIEF

Do you accept? What a loaded question! Do you accept a 1,300-mile move? Do you accept that at twenty-nine years of age you will be the youngest adult in the room? Do you accept the responsibility to lead a church? Do you accept this radical life change? You made a decision to pursue. Now do you accept? "Yes! I accept!"

In the spirit of full transparency and looking back in retrospect, I said yes before I really knew what I was doing. Josie Bisset hit the nail squarely on the head when she said, "Dreams come a size too big so we can grow into them." Some of the greatest moments and achievements in life happen when we risk saying yes before we have the needed skill set or necessary resources. I call this "yes before you're ready." It's like walking a tightrope without a safety net underneath. The yes-before-you're-ready response is the grow-or-die mentality, the response that says, "We didn't move 1,300 miles to quit." We were only twenty-nine years old, but it didn't matter. We said yes before we were ready.

However, I offer this caution: yes-before-you're-ready cannot stand alone. Even as your lips are moving, saying yes to your dreams, you must have a strong urge for action, a hustle-and-grind to close the gap between what you have and what you need. If you're not willing to jump in over your head, sacrifice convenience for the dream, and do whatever it takes, don't say yes.

I recently came across some comment cards about the Bridger Wilderness Area in Wyoming. Originally it was established in 1931 as a primitive area with an incredible range of 428,169 acres. Then, in 1964, the area was redesigned and expanded to its current size. It is home to both grizzly and black bears as well as moose, elk, mule deer, wolverine, bighorn sheep, mountain lions, and wolves. Birds such as bald eagles, osprey, peregrine falcons, and Clark's nutcrackers soar over the acreage. Within its beautiful rivers swim several species of trout, mountain whitefish, and grayling. It also attracts guests who climb its hills, fish in its streams, and sleep under the night sky. Those guests are always invited to share insights from their experiences in the Wyoming wilderness. Here are a few of those responses:

> *Trails need to be wider so people can walk while holding hands.*
>
> *Trails need to be reconstructed. Please avoid building trails that go uphill.*
>
> *Escalators would help on steep uphill sections.*
>
> *Please pave the trails so they can be snow-plowed during the winter.*
>
> *Too many bugs and leeches and spiders and spiderwebs. Please spray the wilderness to rid the areas of these pests.*
>
> *Chairlifts need to be in some places so that we can get to wonderful views without having to hike to them.*
>
> *Coyotes made too much noise last night and kept me awake. Please eradicate these annoying animals.*
>
> *A small deer came into my camp and stole my jar of pickles. Is there a way I can get reimbursed? Please call…*
>
> *Reflectors need to be placed on trees every fifty feet so people can hike at night with flashlights.*
>
> *A McDonald's would be nice at the trailhead.*
>
> *The places where trails do not exist are not well marked.*
>
> *Too many rocks in the mountains.*[3]

What do all of these comments have in common? The people who made them were ready and willing to climb the mountain trails as long as they didn't have to exert too much effort. "Get rid of the rocks, the hills, the spiders, the dark, the coyotes, the deer, and any other problems, then we'll climb the trail." Living out challenging dreams does not just happen. You have to be honest with where you are, know exactly what you want, and be predisposed toward action to close the gap. It involves a heightened sense of urgency, a plan for action, and willingness to royally mess things up—yet still keep going. Even when bloody coats show up at your feet, you gotta keep believing. As you walk the trail of your dreams, you'll come to a point where your belief and commitment are so strong that your dreams become deep-rooted convictions. Many people never develop those convictions because it's easier to be a reed bending in the wind. But that only makes those people appear narrow and intolerant. If you intend to fulfill your dreams, you have to deeply believe in them.

## BELIEF → ACTION

The yes answer to that fateful phone call set off events that would define and redefine our new reality. It launched a month of miracles, events that can only be explained as divine confirmation that we were right where we needed to be. It's amazing how many times we want the miracle *before* we act on our faith. But this journey has taught me that the miracle can only *follow* the act of faith.

Was our saying yes with no guarantee of success any different than Kennedy's declaration "We choose to go to the moon"? Not much. I believe in stretching yourself and giving it everything you've got. Over the next month, there were some awe-inspiring things that took place in our family's lives.

One event happened on the Wednesday I met with a realtor at 11:00 AM and put our Moss Bluff house on the market. We immediately began preparing for a gargantuan two-day garage sale. At 6:00 PM that same day, we received an offer to purchase our home, while allowing our family to stay in the house as needed while I flew to New York to prepare for the big move. I still get teary-eyed thinking about the day we sold our home in less than twenty-four hours. That triggered a domino effect that extended over the next few weeks. Selling our house meant we were debt free; a milestone that we had worked for to help us fulfill our dream of moving to New York. Debt is one of the greatest dream killers. I wonder how many times God requests us to do things, but we can't say yes because of messed-up finances.

We had a financial plan already in place: (1) be 100 percent debt free, and (2) have three to six month's income in savings. The action I took to accomplish that was to get a second temporary job. Walt Disney said, "The future is not the result of choices among alternative paths offered in the present. It is a place created—created first in the mind and will; created next in activity."[4]

## ACTION → REALITY

That sounds like rainbows and unicorns, but after we moved to New York on April 1, 2017, we found out there is a dark side to dreams. There was no "honeymoon stage"; it was rough from the start. We decided that Ashley would finish teaching the school year in Louisiana, and she and the kids would join me in June. In the interim, I began to house hunt while staying in an apartment on Long Island, which was over an hour from Valhalla. By the time Ashley and the kids joined me, I was living in a hotel in Stamford, Connecticut. We were jammed in that tiny hotel room for nearly three months. Life in a small hotel room with a three-year-old and a six-month-old is not exactly a picnic. Stress levels were at an all-time high not only because of the living situation, but also because of the steep learning curve as pastor. It seemed like I messed things up on a daily basis. Conflict was the order of the day and everything was a headache. It became overwhelming.

We were groping our way through an emotional fog. Thankfully, we had mentors and friends, people whom we trust to speak into our life and friends with whom we felt safe to share our honest thoughts. Having a small group of mentors reaped great benefits when conflict arose. One of the greatest things you can do to ensure the fulfillment of your dream is to surround yourself with people you trust and then listen when they speak. These people have already walked the path and can invest wisdom and knowledge into your life. Over time, the gaps between conflicts began to widen. I remember making phone calls to those trusted mentors and saying things like, "Well, I messed up only once this week . . . things are getting better!"

By the time we finally moved into our new home, we had spent every penny to our name—literally. Financially broke, emotionally exhausted, and physically ill with frequent trips to urgent care, I came nose to nose with the brutal realization we had no choice but to succeed. When there are a million reasons to quit—to let that crazy dream keel over and die—that's when you remember it's not a dream anymore; it's now your belief. It's your conviction. Saying yes means you have the fortitude to make your dream become a reality.

Many people won't understand your dream. People who don't know you will one day see you as an overnight success, not recognizing the years and decades you spent in agonizing prayer, research, determination, vision, and bloody coats. That's all right. Keep dreaming, believing, daring, doing, and investing.

One last addendum to this story is that in 2009 I had preached a youth weekend at Westchester Church. I remember standing at the back of the church auditorium thinking, *I want to believe and invest in something like this!* So, for the next decade, never imagining I would end up pastoring Westchester Church, we began sending a financial gift to the church every month. I wrote in my journal, "Like planted seeds, we've invested in the ground, and it's about to rain!"

Here is a principle: Your dream is the seed. The rain will come, but it can only help grow what is already planted. The greatest dreams are ones that cost you. If it's a "cheap" dream, more than likely it won't amount to much. You have to make a covenant with yourself and be willing to invest everything to see that dream come true. Over time you will reap a harvest. "Most assuredly, I say to you, unless a grain of wheat falls into the ground and dies, it remains alone; but if it dies, it produces much grain" (John 12:24, NKJV).

*A Note from Ashley, taken from her message at a ladies' event:*

> *Donny's childhood pastor used to say that people make finding the will of God harder than it is. He would say, "The will of God is simple; just bloom where you're planted!" That phrase has stuck with me throughout the seasons of my life. Several years ago, I was shopping at Target and saw a sign on the $1 aisle that said, "Bloom where you're planted!" I had heard Pastor Mahoney say that, so I bought it. My plan was to frame it and hang it with some other stuff I had, but I never got around to it. That sign languished in the back of my craft closet for years. However, it did make the cut of things to bring to New York.*
>
> *Fast forward a year to September, when I took a teaching job. I couldn't stir up any excitement about that job, but it was clearly a God thing, so I decided to take it. Honestly, I was having a hard time juggling everything: a new baby, caring for two older kids, running the house-hold, and helping Donny with church things.*
>
> *In the past I've spent at a least a week getting my classroom ready for the new school year. This time I had only a few hours on a Saturday because we had a lot of other things going on that weekend. I hurriedly grabbed several boxes of stuff out my craft closet—any-thing I thought I might use in my classroom. I finally*

*settled into the new job, but I was exhausted and overwhelmed. I think I did a good job, but the passion wasn't there. I would rather have been home taking care of my babies or planning events for Westchester Church. This job was the last thing on my list of priorities, and I was always so ready to leave at the end of the day.*

*I finally unpacked the box with the "bloom" sign in it and was immediately convicted. I could be pouring so much more into my job. Now I have the sign tacked right by my desk to remind me that even though I didn't choose to be planted here, this is where God planted me so I might as well enjoy it and bloom! I figure that while I'm here I'm going to pray that God will help me be the best I can be. Since then, I have enjoyed my job so much more. So my advice to you is just to "Bloom where you're planted!"*

*Side note:* A year after Ashley spoke on this subject, she became principal of her school and is still blooming where she was planted.

## THREE BIG IDEAS

1. Do dreams automatically come true? No, you have to engage in the process. The bigger the dream the greater attention must be paid to the process. Good intentions are never enough. There must be a systematic process and picture inside of your head that compel you to move forward.

2. The growth cycle of a Dream = Thought → Decision → Belief → Action → Reality

3. Bloom where you're planted!

## THREE BIG QUESTIONS

1. Dreams become thoughts. What are you thinking about your dreams right now?

   _____

   _____

2. What is one decision you can make today concerning your thoughts?

   _____

   _____

3. Write what you want your life to look like ten years from now.

   _____

   _____

# CHARACTERISTICS OF A DREAMER

*"The poor man is not he who is without a cent,*
*but he who is without a dream!" –Harry Kemp*

What are the characteristics of a successful dreamer? Do they possess a certain DNA? What does success look like? We could discuss a wide variety of characteristics, but I'd like to highlight a few that really matter: ethics, concrete purpose, defined principle, and consistency. These characteristics, when incorporated into our everyday lives, are the tools that will lead us to success. The lives of dreamers who lack these characteristics are like the ball in a pinball machine. You pull back the plunger and let it go, then it's bells, whistles, flippers, and down the hole. There's a whole lot of noise and no direction. The ball bounces from situation to situation, then makes a quick exit.

The story is told of an elderly Sicilian priest who was sitting in the stern of a rowboat, being rowed across the river by a ferryman. Watching the ferryman bend over the oars, the priest asked, "Tell me, my good man, have you studied any philosophy?" The ferryman answered, "No, no philosophy." "A pity," the priest replied. "You've wasted a quarter of your life." The ferryman kept rowing. The priest asked, "What about history? Have you studied that?" "No," said the ferryman, "I didn't study no history." "What a shame," said the priest, "you've wasted half your life." The ferryman kept rowing. "What about mathematics?" asked the priest. "Surely you've learned some mathematics!" "Nope," said the ferryman, "no mathematics." "A tragedy," said the priest. "You've wasted three-fourths of your life." Halfway across the river the ferryman looked down and saw water filling the bottom of the boat. "Tell me, Father," he said. "Have you learned how to swim?" "Why, no," said the priest. "A pity," said the ferryman. "You've wasted all your life."[1]

## ETHICS

After the discovery of the Enron corruption scheme, a book publisher approached John Maxwell about publishing a book on business ethics. Maxwell told the publishers he couldn't do it. When they asked him why, he said that there was no such thing as business ethics—only ethics. If a person lives by a code of ethics, it will show up in every area of their life, not just in business. An ethical person will exhibit qualities like integrity, attitude, caring, excellence, honesty, and the courage to stand up for what is right.

I once came across the story of the Rockdale County High School Bulldogs basketball team out of Conyers, Georgia. Cleveland Stroud had coached the team for eighteen years without winning a state championship, but he had a good feeling about the 1987 season. Catching his enthusiasm, the school installed a glass cabinet in the gym to display the expected trophy. Stroud's feeling proved correct; they went 22–5 during the season and won a blowout victory, earning their first-ever state championship.

Two months after the season ended, Coach Stroud was conducting a routine review of his players' grades when he discovered that one of his third-string players had failed some courses, rendering him ineligible to play. During one of the semifinal matches, with the Bulldogs ahead by twenty points, the coach had decided to give every player a chance to participate. The ineligible player was in the game for only forty-five seconds. He scored no points, and his participation did not affect the outcome of the game. Coach Stroud now faced a dilemma. If he kept quiet about his discovery, chances were no one would ever discover the mistake and the Bulldog trophy could stay in the cabinet. If he revealed the mistake, the team would be stripped of its state championship and the trophy taken away.

The coach said later, "We didn't know he was ineligible at the time. In fact, we didn't know it until a few weeks ago. Some people have said we should have just kept quiet about it, that it was just forty-five seconds, and the player wasn't an impact player. But you've got to do what is honest and right and what the rules say. I told my team that people will forget the scores of basketball games, but they don't forget what you're made of."[2] That's ethics.

A few years back I was in a situation that affected a lot of people, which forced me to make a hard choice. A certain individual had helped us tremendously for over a year, and for that we were grateful. But a lot of times when someone does something for you for free, you usually discover there are strings attached. Some of the strings are no big deal—others are really big deals. We got into a situation where I had to make a decision between my convictions and a convenience. The blessing had become a curse and there was some tension in the relationship that unfortunately was irreconcilable, so I made the phone call (it did not go well) and I broke off the partnership. It was a choice to end a very powerful and lucrative business relationship.

Later that evening my wife reminded me of the verse of Scripture that says, "A person may think their own ways are right, but the LORD weighs the heart" (Proverbs 21:2, NIV). As I pondered this verse, it hit me that there was no way to prove I was wrong, and no way to prove the other party was wrong. We were both right in our own eyes, and, quite frankly, nothing would change that. But the Lord wasn't looking for proofs; He was looking at our hearts.

My actions were correct in my own eyes, but I didn't want my "rightness" to become righteous indignation. It leads to bitterness, and bitterness is deadly. It breeds deep loathing, hatred, bad blood, and malice. It kills joy, hope, and relationships. We must protect ourselves from bitterness, because, like a pandemic, it's contagious and destructive.

Bitterness is the absence of forgiveness. If you dwell on the wrong done to you, you are giving power to the other person. Their actions control your thoughts, your emotions, and your sleeping habits. If you don't let them go, every relationship in your life will be infected. When conflicts arise, we must forgive gracefully and let go quickly. Carrying hurt and bitterness is like you swallowing rat poison and expecting the other individual to die. It does nothing but hurt you and the ones closest to you. No person can be bitter and keep it to him or herself.

When the coat gets bloody, we must remember not only what we want, but also be able to control our spirit and attitude.

Good character requires an element of self-control, the ability to keep emotions and actions together, like two rails on a train track. Research suggests that those who can control their emotions and actions end up better off from almost any point of view. They are happier, healthier, have better relationships, make more money, and go further in their careers. They deal with stress and conflict better, and even live longer.

As I stated in my intro, I am a father of three, and during the 2020 quarantine they were ages six, three, and two. Our streaming service, *Disney+*, released *Frozen 2*, a movie that includes a song that highlights the topic of values. The song "Do the Next Right Thing" says, "Just do the next right thing. Take a step, step again."

That's what I call ethics. Talent and ability will take a person to the top, but ethics will keep them there. Ethics will refuse to give in to pressure. Ethics won't go with the flow. Ethics will dissent in the face of adverse popular opinion. Whatever your dream is, make sure it's built on ethics. Anything less will come tumbling down like a house of cards.

## CONCRETE PURPOSE

Concrete purpose answers the question of why you are here. You were made for a purpose. However, I believe that the idea of purpose can be deceiving. Talking about purpose sometimes comes across as unicorns and rainbows. But really, it's the complete opposite. It's a deep belief in something you are willing to do. It's doing the hard things over and over again. It's accepting help, criticism, and constructive criticism, because your "why" is more important than what you feel or what you experience. Put purpose over feeling. Put purpose over pain. Put purpose over insecurity. Thomas Carlyle said, "The man without a purpose is like a ship without a rudder—a waif, a nothing, a no man. Have a purpose in life, and having it, throw such strength of mind and muscle into your work as God has given you."[3]

The greatest tragedy is not death, but a life lived without purpose. Nothing matters more than knowing the purpose for your life, and nothing can compensate for not knowing it—not success, wealth, fame, or pleasure. Without purpose, life becomes trivial, petty, and pointless. Like treading water, it becomes activity without direction, and events without reason. When life is meaningless and insignificant and hopeless, people will continually change directions, jobs, relationships, churches, or other externals, hoping each change will settle the confusion or fill the emptiness in their heart. They convince themselves that maybe this time it will be different, but in reality, it simply delays the inevitable and doesn't solve the real problem—a lack of focus and purpose. "Don't live carelessly, unthinkingly. Make sure you understand what the Master wants" (Ephesians 5:17, *The Message*).

On the other hand, a person with purpose knows why they are here, and that knowledge enables them to change their world. When situations get uncomfortable, they remember why they made the decisions in the first place. We were not created to just exist from day to day with no real direction or fulfillment in life. We were created according to a grand design. One of the most effective leaders in the Bible, the apostle Paul, said, "I am focusing all my energies on this one thing: forgetting the past and looking forward to what lies ahead." He never lost sight of his purpose and methodically walked toward it.

## DEFINED PRINCIPLE

A quick Google search on "Living by Principle" will tell you there are millions of different views on the topic. Headlines such as, "5 principles to live by," "3 principles that will change your life," "101 principles you need to succeed"—you name it, it's there. If you try to live by them all, you'll be bouncing around like that pinball. The most disappointing article I read was one that declared living by principles is a negative. I could not disagree more. I believe we must live not only by principle but by *defined* principle. Why defined? Because definition brings clarity.

Think of "defined principle" as the canvas of your life. Principle provides the frame, the boundaries within which you have the luxury to paint and create. Those boundaries are your constant. Some say principles make life predictable. That's true. The cause-and-effect of principle creates the potential for predictable outcomes. However, life without principle would be random. Principles are what enable us to plan with some element of confidence. Just as you dare not ignore the principle of gravity, prudence tells you not to ignore the principle of life, which is this: it is *direction* and not intention that determines *destination*.

What do these boundaries look like in real time? Consider this: Every January people make New Year's resolutions. They set goals for the year—health goals, financial goals, relationship goals, you get the picture. I used to be an avid goal-setter, but recently I've begun viewing it differently. While the world was making New Year's resolutions, I began to define three principles I wanted to live by daily. These would be three things I could apply to any situation or decision over the course of the year. Every decision and opportunity during that year must correspond with those three principles. Change is inevitable; situations change and stages of life change. But guiding principles are the North Star of a person navigating through life. No one else gets to determine your guiding principles; you are the principle-setter.

To illustrate, let me walk you through the three principles for the year 2020: (1) pray more, (2) eliminate distractions, and (3) be extra. Sometimes after I preach my wife will say, "Donny, your sermon was good, but you need to offer real-time examples." So the following section shows what these principles mean and how they look in real time. At the end of this chapter you'll have a chance to define your guiding principles. Here are mine.

## PRAY MORE

When speaking to the National Wild Turkey Federation, the late Supreme Court Justice Antonin Scalia revealed one of the reasons why he loved hunting: "Those of us who are religious—and most turkey hunters, in my experience, are—value that time alone. There's just something spiritual about it. You can pray to the Creator out there, even while you're hunting."

Prayer is not just talking to the ceiling (though sometimes it may feel that way). Prayer is the greatest source of direction. It provides opportunity to step away from the clutter of life, take a deep breath, clear your mind, and get your bearings.

*In real time:* There is something special about waking up early and, in the quietness of the morning, speaking to the One who hung the earth upon nothing. There's a special serenity, maybe because I know that within a few hours my three children will bounce out of bed and peace will be gone. Prayer accesses wisdom and broadens my perspective. Prayer shows me that I'm simply a small piece of a great puzzle of life, and gives me the opportunity to consider how I can best add value to the puzzle. Psalm 19:14 has been a strong anchor in my life: "Let the words of my mouth, and the meditation of my heart, be acceptable in thy sight, O LORD, my strength, and my redeemer." I want my words, my heart, and my meditation to be acceptable to the Lord. I've always prayed, but I want to pray more.

## ELIMINATE DISTRACTIONS

Distractions bound out of everywhere throughout the twenty-four hours of every day. Some you can't avoid; others, you must avoid. That's why it's important to know when to say yes when to say no—and the wisdom to know how to say it. "No" can be said in a number of different ways; sometimes it's a loud hyper-bold no, sometimes it's an apologetic but firm no. Yeses can eliminate distractions. Sometimes it's saying yes to someone who wants out of a situation. Or it's a yes to someone offering to take something off of your plate. Whatever the form, eliminating distractions opens the door to more productivity and creativity.

A sign frequently seen on everything from wall plaques to coffee mugs reflects a quote by Hilary Cooper: "Life is not measured by the breaths you take but the number of moments that took your breath away." It's not just that you live; it's the kind of life you live. When you're overcommitted with distractions you can't function at your best. Don't be afraid to eliminate. Keep life simple.

*In real time:* If you open the app store on your phone, you'll see dozens of time-management and time-saver applications that offer productive shortcuts and to-do lists to help you stay on course. Call me old school, but I still use paper and pencil. While to-do lists are needful, they should also be managed. If they're not managed, your day will become consumed with tasks that do not move you toward your ultimate goal. Bob Hawke, prime minister of Australia, said, "The things which are most important don't always scream the loudest."[4] Many times, our days become a checklist of things to do rather than a focus on things that matter. Award-winning business journalist Emma Johnson offered the following tips to eliminate distractions and stay focused:

1. Stop digital pressures. Carve out blocks of time—whether for work, exercise or people you care about—and turn off your phone and computer.

2. Give yourself frequent breaks. Just because you can work 24/7 doesn't mean your mind or body are designed to do so.

3. Mind your physical health. Exercise, plenty of sleep, healthy eating and all of those things you know you're supposed to do promote mental health and focus.

4. Turn off smartphone notifications. Limit the number of times per day you check and respond to email, texts and social media. Remove the temptation to constantly keep an eye on these pests.

5. Knock out the most dreaded duties first thing in the morning. Have a difficult email you must send? Bills to manage? Need to initiate a difficult conversation? Get it off your to-do list and out of your mind, freeing you to be productive.

6. Eliminate or minimize negative people in your life. These are people who play the victim, are stuck in unhealthy habits, or generally make you feel drained or bad about yourself. Surround yourself with those who are positive, focused, productive and ambitious. Remember the late iconic speaker Jim Rohn's rule: "You are the average of the five people you spend the most time with."[5]

One last thought on eliminating distractions. We live in a day in which we're told to educate ourselves and be better informed. But it isn't the mere accumulation of information that is important. Knowledge can be a distraction. What is relevant today will be irrelevant tomorrow. I still remember downloading the internet from a floppy disk! If that confuses you, google "AOL floppy disk" and you'll get a picture of those olden days compared to today. Knowledge of specific subjects will fade. Philosophy will get challenged. Plans will change. But concrete principles will never fade. They are the borders of your everyday life.

## BE EXTRA—SAY YES!

*Dear Optimist, Pessimist, and Realist,*
    *While you were busy arguing about the glass of [water],*
*I drank it!*
        *Sincerely,*
        *The Opportunist*[6]

When I think of being "extra," I think of new opportunities. Our English word *opportunity* comes from the Latin word meaning "toward the port." It suggests a ship taking advantage of the winds and tides to arrive safely in the harbor. The brevity of life is a strong argument for making the best use of the opportunities we have.

People who look for opportunities usually find them. For instance, Richard Branson, the boss of Virgin Airlines, was with a group of journalists during the dedication of the company's inaugural flight to Los Angeles. They were staying at a first-class hotel, and the journalists were all in the lobby waiting for a limo to take them back to the airport. A young female journalist approached Branson and asked him the secret formula for making money. He responded, "Just keep your eyes open and the answer jumps right at you. Look at those outdoor heaters the hotel has around the pool, for example. I've never seen them before, and with the English weather the way it is, I'd bet they would sell like hot cakes at home. Find out who makes them and see if you can get the UK distribution rights." The woman checked it out and was told she could buy the rights for $3,000. She didn't bother. A few years later, the company that bought those rights was sold for $25 million. Opportunities are endless for people who keep their eyes open and their mind on being extra.

Time ushers in opportunity and closes the door on opportunity. It is the vehicle by which we travel from moment to moment. Time is a nonspatial continuum in which events occur in apparently irreversible succession from the past through the present and into the future. It has been said that time is life; thus, to waste time is to waste life. You don't have a guarantee of even one more day to live.

I'm a person who tends to say yes. On the other hand, I have certain friends who, when asked for a favor, will automatically say no, so I've stopped asking. The reason I say yes is (1) I enjoy helping people and (2) I like it when people say yes to me, as in "Do unto others . . ." So, if I can say yes, I will. I believe saying yes could be the door to a new opportunity.

*In real time:* For the most part, Ashley and I are creatures of habit. At the beginning of every month we sit down for our calendar meeting and everything we discuss is placed in one of three categories: (1) priority, (2) necessity, and (3) extra. We figure out what we desire to say yes to and what we feel is worthy of our time. Here is what it looks like:

*Schedule priorities first.* As Ashley and I plan our monthly calendar, we write in the things we value most before scheduling anything else. One of the things we value most is quality family time. For example, a few months back I received an email requesting me to speak at a meeting on the first Saturday of the month. However, every first Saturday of the month from nine to noon is Home Depot's Kids Workshop, held in stores across the country. The kids receive a free project kit, kid-sized orange apron, and a commemorative pin they can put on their apron. Since our kids are our priority, the first thing we write on the calendar is "Home Depot" on the first Saturday of the month. It's not penciled in; it's etched in stone. Why does the Kids Workshop matter so much to us? It's not the purpose; it's simply the tool we are using to fulfill our purpose, which is to forge strong relationships with our children. Yes, the event is fun and exciting, but there's a futuristic truth lodged in the back of my mind. The day will come when my kids won't want to go to the workshop, but that's all right because they still will want to spend time with me. The priorities in our lives such as church, family time, and events that are important to us are scheduled first.

*What about extra?* Second, we schedule work and school-related activities—the necessities that can't be put off. That's self-explanatory. But I want to call attention to the third category—extra. "Extra" really can't be scheduled. These are the things that just come up, stuff you didn't expect. Sometimes it's an emergency. Sometimes it's another person's emergency. We know "extra" is going to occur, but where does it fit into the calendar? Is there any way we can prepare for the unknown? I believe the answer is yes. Step back from the calendar, look at it as a whole, and you'll notice plenty of blank spaces. Ashley and I call that the "space margin." The space margin gets packed with the extra stuff that can consume both time and things. It can put a squeeze on *necessity* to the point where necessities do not receive the attention they deserve. The extras can even elbow their way past the priorities. I'm sure we are not the only people who know what this looks like. So how do we manage? The answer is to be realistic about how much time things take and schedule the extra margin as an event.

*In real time:* You're sitting down at the dinner table with your calendar and a cup of coffee, formulating your monthly plan. Every foreseen event has been categorized. You've created reasonable margins of time, and you're feeling really good about it. Then midway through the month, an extra opportunity arises. That's the time to say yes.

## CONSISTENCY

The last characteristic that is vital to the makeup of a dreamer is consistency. Consider the grass and how it grows. Dew brings growth even though it comes silently and unnoticed. We cannot depend on the consistency of the rain, but we can depend on the consistency of the dew. Growth doesn't come from the big loud storm. There are two stories that I believe paint the best picture of consistency.

*Consistency—The South Pole.* Jim Collins included in his book *Great by Choice* an illustration that has shaped my views on consistency, on bringing dreams to reality, and on life in general. The story is of two explorers, Amundsen and Scott, who, in 1911, led two different teams in an expedition race to the South Pole and back. This race was equivalent to a round-trip distance from New York City to South Louisiana, roughly 1,400 miles. Both teams would travel the same distance through the same weather, conditions, environments, and opportunities. The difference came in the approach.

Robert Scott, a British Navy officer, based his team's entire approach on weather. On days that were bright with good visibility, his team would march as far as possible. But on days with harsh conditions or limited visibility, they rested and conserved their energy.

Roald Amundsen, a Norwegian explorer, took a totally different approach with his team. He dismissed weather as irrelevant. It didn't matter if the weather or visibility was good or bad, he was determined to march twenty miles every day. I can almost hear the conversation in the morning: "OK, team, today we move forward another twenty miles." "But Mr. Amundsen, it's clear and sunny. Why not try for forty miles?" or "It's dark and rainy with no visibility. Can we just relax today?" To which Amundsen would reply, "Yesterday we walked twenty miles. Today we will walk twenty miles. Tomorrow we will walk twenty miles." Can you guess which team won the expedition? I think you can: the team that consistently pressed forward, the team that marched twenty miles every day. That was their standard and they stuck to it. They were consistent.

*Consistency—The North Star.* One of my favorite American History stories took place during the height of the Underground Railroad movement prior to the Civil War. Harriet Tubman, the best-known conductor of the Underground Railroad, roused many enslaved Americans in the South to seek freedom in the North. Night travel afforded the best chance of escaping; however, most slaves did not have maps or compasses to guide them. Without the use of these tools, a fugitive's ability to successfully navigate in the dark to a safe house, railroad station, or the woods was often a matter of life or death. So they were told to follow the North Star. To find that star they were to first find the "drinking gourd" (you may know it as the Big Dipper). Using the distance between the two stars on the outermost edge of the dipper, they were told to draw a continuous straight line stretching five times that distance. That imaginary line would connect to the North Star. If the stars were obscured by clouds, they needed to remember that moss grows on the north side of the trees. Most slaves couldn't read or write, but "reading" the night sky provided important clues for survival.

The Big Dipper and the North Star were referenced in many slave narratives and songs. "Follow the Drinking Gourd" was a popular African-American folksong composed decades after the War and based on these anecdotes that memorialized the significance of these stars.

> *When the sun come back,*
> *And the firs' quail calls,*
> *Then the time is come.*
> *Foller the drinkin gou'd.*

These early Americans staked their freedom on a star, an immovable object. We too should set our lives on immovable principles. In the Shakespearean play *Julius Caesar*, Brutus says, "I am as constant as the North Star." Of course, Brutus was more of a wandering star than a constant star, but for those who track stars, most stars appear to wander across the heavens as the earth orbits. But not the North Star. In relation to earth, it remains perfectly still. Time exposures reveal that the North Star remains constant while all the other stars seem to swirl about. From that fixed point, ancient mariners navigated the watery highways of the sea, and passengers on the Underground Railroad made their way from slavery to freedom. And a fixed-point dream can go from a thought to a reality. Consistency matters.

## FOUR BIG IDEAS

1. Ethics Matter. Ability and talent will take a man to the top, and ethics will keep him there. Ethical people refuse to give in to pressure. They don't go with the flow; they will dissent even when going against the tide of popular opinion. Whatever your dream or desire may be, make sure it's built on ethics. Anything less is as rickety as a house of cards.

2. Concrete Purpose. Your *why* is more important than *what* you feel or experience. Place purpose over feeling, over pain, and over insecurity. Place purpose over everything.

3. Defined Principle. I define a guiding principle as "a priority with which every decision and opportunity must agree." Situations change and stages of life change, but what guides me is constant.

4. Power of Consistency. The North Star remains constant while all the other stars swirl about. From that fixed point, ancient mariners navigated the highways of the sea, and passengers on the Underground Railroad made their way from slavery to freedom. Fixing on an unmovable point, your dream can go from a thought to a reality.

## THREE BIG QUESTIONS

1. What is your purpose?

   _____

   _____


2. What are your principles?

   _____

   _____


3. What is your plan this month to fulfill your purpose?

   _____

   _____

| Priorities | Necessities | EXTRA |
| --- | --- | --- |
|  |  |  |

# Part 2
## GOOD!

The intent of the first section of this book was to lay a foundation. In this "Good!" section, we will delve into the principles of the growth cycle of a dream. We'll discuss thoughts, actions, beliefs, and realities—basic elements of the dream. I invite you to engage with me in this conversation by marking up the book and writing notes in the margins. It could change your life; I know it did mine. Challenge your thinking about where your life is and where you want it to be.

# Part 2

## GOOD!

# GOOD THOUGHTS

*"For as he thinketh in his heart, so is he." (Proverbs 23:7)*

Thoughts are the fundamental level of a dream's origin. Everything begins with a simple thought. "I think . . ." "I think I can." "What do you think about it?" If thoughts are so important, where do they originate from? How many thoughts does a person have in a day? What thoughts should be kept and what thoughts should be cast out? All of these questions affect a person's goals and desires, because, as Solomon wisely said, thoughts are the essence of what a person will become. Please allow me to begin this section of the book by quoting Dr. Seuss, one of my favorite authors:

*Congratulations!*
*Today is your day.*
*You're off to Great Places!*
*You're off and away!*
*You have brains in your head.*
*You have feet in your shoes.*
*You can steer yourself*
*Any direction you choose.*
*You're on your own. And you know what you know.*
*And YOU are the guy who'll decide where to go.*[1]

My favorite line is "You have brains in your head." That's the gray matter encased in your skull. It's your Grand Central Terminal that interprets all incoming sensory information from the world around you and controls all your bodily systems with lightning impulses along an intricate network of nerves. Doctors can pinpoint specific areas of the brain that control various functions of your body. Google "regions of the brain and what they control," and you'll see diagrams with acupuncture-like needles labeled "concentration/problem-solving," "motor control," "language," "hearing," or "facial recognition." I find it amazing that inside your skull is a three-pound organ that has more stored information than the Library of Congress with its seventeen million volumes!

Scientists have tried to guess how many thoughts an individual thinks per day. Estimates range from six thousand to eighty thousand. One leading scientist had 184 volunteers sit down and watch movies. Using a mysterious new method called fMRI, he claimed he could identify "thought worms"—moments when a person is focused on a specific idea. He could figure out not *what* the volunteers were thinking, but *when* they were thinking about one idea and *when* they moved on to a new idea. His conclusion was that people think, on average, six thousand thoughts per day. My point is that the thought process remains a mystery to scientists, but one thing is not a mystery: *your life is shaped by your thoughts*.

Michigan State University Extension's "Stress Less with Mindfulness" program posits that a person has eighty thousand thoughts a day. Ninety percent of these thoughts are ones we have had before, and 80 percent of these are negative.[2] What a staggering statistic! If true, this means that only 20 percent of your thoughts are positive, and a mere 10 percent will be original. These statistics may be the reason why so many dreams go unfulfilled. We tell ourselves things like "Get your head out of the clouds. Daydreams don't amount to anything. Be logical. Be smart. You don't really want that. You should feel ashamed for thinking those things. Stop acting selfishly. You shouldn't aim that high." In all the negativity, we accept limitations because our thoughts are neither positive nor even right. It's not good and it's not healthy.

Here's an idea for you: Sit alone in a quiet room. While thinking positive thoughts, begin to make a list of your dreams. Believe it or not, there is incredible power in writing things down. It takes work to find that 10 percent of original thoughts and that 20 percent of positive thoughts. That's why creativity and new ideas come at such a premium.

## THE RIGHT MINDSET

The old saying goes, "If you think you can or if you think you can't, you are correct." Mindset matters. Why does it seem the universe is tilted in favor of some people? Why do others seem to have the golden touch or have the knack to finish first? Tom Brady won six Super Bowl titles in the National Football League. Michael Jordan won six national championships in basketball. Serena Williams won thirty-nine titles overall in tennis—twenty-three singles, fourteen doubles, and two mixed doubles titles. College football coach Nick Saban won five national championships.

Some people are winners. But why? The more I read of these individuals the more convinced I am that they have a winning mindset. Their minds have a level of expectation and they know what to do with it.

I recently heard a speaker tell the story of a man named Carlos Hathcock, who was a sniper for the United States Army. Even if the target was over a mile away, he could hit it. During the Vietnam conflict he had over ninety-three confirmed kills. At the end of his career he was asked to do one more mission that would require him to crawl two thousand yards through a field. He said, "There ain't a stitch of cover within two thousand yards of that place. I've got the tree line for cover up to here," his finger tapped the circle as he spoke. "All I'm gonna get at the guy is one shot. I can't gamble on connecting at a thousand yards—it's gotta be eight hundred yards or less. That means I've gotta cover about fifteen hundred yards of open ground without being seen."[3]

He began his homework. He surveyed aerial photographs of the area and determined there was a shallow gully he could crawl into and take the kill shot at eight hundred yards. He packed no food, just a small canteen of water and his Model 70 Winchester rifle. When he reached the edge of the tree line, Hathcock lay on his side and inched his way across the open field, taking three days to crawl a thousand yards through grass barely a foot above his head. He never slept for fear of snoring, never stopped except when the North Vietnamese walked through the field looking for threats. Ants crawled over his skin. His tongue stuck to the roof of his mouth. Constantly moving at a snail's pace, he finally reached his spot, methodically calculating the light, humidity, breeze, and air density, and how all of these factors would affect the velocity of his bullet. Finally, he squeezed the trigger. Never being noticed, he dropped back into the gully and crawled out of the area, reaching the safety zone three days later. When asked about his successful mission, he commented, "When I planned the mission I was in my right mind."[4]

In his book *How Good Do You Want to Be?* Coach Nick Saban suggests five ways to have a winning mindset: (1) Invest your time; don't spend it. (2) You won't always get what you want, but you always get what you deserve. (3) Promise a starting time, but not a quitting time. (4) Patience is necessary for success. (5) Enjoy your work.[5]

## POSITIVE IMAGINATION

The first knockdown of Muhammad Ali's professional boxing career was in the fifteenth round in the ring with Joe Frazier. In the eleventh round, Frazier threw a left hook, causing Ali to stumble around the ring. By the fourteenth round, Frazier could hardly see through swollen eyes. At the start of the fifteenth round, Frazier was ahead. Ali had just set up an uppercut when a right hook smashed into his face. Down he went. Amazingly, he popped back up, but his fate was sealed and Frazier was announced as the winner by unanimous vote. An interviewer asked Ali why he had jumped back up, and he responded, "The first thing I heard was 'eight.' The first thing I thought was 'I don't belong here.'" He got up and finished the fight. He was a champion, and champions don't belong on the ground.

Psychologist Terry Orlick determined that one of the common traits among champions was "positive imagination." For example, before a world-class sprinter lines up to run a hundred-meter sprint, he has already won the race in his mind. He envisions the start, sprint, and finish before he takes the first stride. A basketball player sees himself hitting in a shooting zone for a game and pictures himself launching the game-winning shot. All-Star baseball players visualize the pitch, the swing, and the ball sailing out of the park. Before you will ever succeed, you must see yourself having that success, because positive imagination leads to positive results.

## MANAGED INTAKE

Your days are filled with constant exposure to social media, movies, books, network news, and the people around you. Due to intake of constant exposure, your thoughts will determine your self-identity, your relationships, and your mental and physical health. It all begins with your thoughts—happy or sad, good or bad, carnal or spiritual. It's important to regulate your intake—the content you consume. How did you learn to rattle off the multiplication tables or the states and their capitals? How did you learn song lyrics or memorize poetry? Repetition! What you put into your mind repeatedly will occupy it. What occupies your mind will ultimately express itself in your lifestyle.

Having thoughts is not the problem; it's managing those thoughts. "Managing your intake" is the ability to consume information and ideas in a way that doesn't throw your emotions into chaos. Each day we are bombarded with so much information and other input that it becomes overwhelming. I'm not advocating being uninformed or uneducated, nor am I referencing tunnel vision. I'm not implying that you can't determine what information is helpful and what information is not. Managed intake is the power to make informed decisions without the emotional baggage that others attempt to pile on you. Whether the information is "right" or "wrong," it's how you respond to that information that makes a difference. Harvey Firestone, a successful businessman of the late nineteenth and early twentieth century said, "Capital isn't so important in business. Experiences aren't so important. You can get both of these things. What is important is ideas. If you have ideas you have the main asset you need, and there isn't any limit to what you can do with your business and your life. They are any man's greatest asset—ideas."[6]

Considering that 80 percent of your thoughts are negative and 90 percent are repetitive, it's important to restructure your thought life to produce new and positive thoughts, to become a positive person with new outlooks. The more ideas you gather and test, the more likely you are to find the ones that work. Just as there isn't only one right answer to most problems, there isn't just one good idea. There are many. One last point on thought intake: thoughts are going to fly over your head, and there's nothing you can do about it. But you can choose to let them go or let them lodge there. Choose wisely.

## THREE BIG IDEAS

1. Everything begins as a thought, so *how you think gives definition to your life*. You have anywhere from six thousand to eighty thousand thoughts per day. Ninety percent of these thoughts are repetitive, and 80 percent are negative.

2. We need to manage our thought intake, because one negative thought can sour the day. On the other hand, one good thought can make for a great day!

3. It's important to restructure your thought life in order to produce new and positive thoughts, to become a positive person with fresh outlooks. Therefore, place very high value on new ideas and thoughts.

## THREE BIG QUESTIONS

1. Write three things that you think about yourself. Are these thoughts a part of the 80 percent negative or 20 percent positive?

   _____

   _____

2. Managed Intake. What are some things you need to toss out of your life in order to focus on the important things?

_____

_____

3. Winning Mindset. What do you see yourself winning at?

_____

_____

6

# Good Decisions

*"The moment you doubt whether you can fly, you cease for ever to be able to do it."* -J.M. Barrie[1]

I'm guessing you know some people who couldn't make a decision if their life depended on it. You want to say, "Hey, just decide already!" This thought has crossed my mind a gazillion times as I smile and simply wait for the decision-maker to decide. I used to be less wise. I would jump in and make the decision for them, until I learned doing that can be a turn-off.

Making the right decision can be difficult. If everything was clearly good or evil, right or wrong, you say, "What's the big fuss? This is simple." But in the real world, we have to make decisions that are multidimensional. I guarantee that life will present moments when you are forced to make a decision, and the right thing isn't obvious.

Life is full of decisions—according to *Psychology Today*, you might make, on average, 35,000 decisions per day. Many times you hesitate when making those decisions because you don't know the outcome. You stand at the crossroads and strain your eyes to see as far as you can. If you take the left fork, then "this" might happen. If you take the right fork, then "that" might happen. You consult the experts, talk to your mentor, or google for solutions, striving to see as far down the road as possible. You ask yourself, "Is this a good decision?" You can either be prudent and attempt to make the best decision with the information you have, or you can become paralyzed by fear and indecision. The step between prudence and fear is short and steep. Prudence climbs in the car and snaps on the safety belt; fear won't even get in the car. Prudence washes with soap and disinfectant; fear avoids human contact. Prudence saves for old age; fear hoards everything—even trash. Prudence prepares and plans; fear panics. Prudence calculates the risk and takes the plunge; fear won't even stick a toe in the water. The more meaningful the decision, the greater chance of conflict and cost.

On June 5, 1944, General Dwight Eisenhower wrote a statement, folded it up, and placed it in his wallet. The short statement acknowledged the iffy outcome of Operation Overlord, also known as D-Day. It said,

> Our landings in the Cherbourg-Havre area have failed to gain a satisfactory foothold and I have withdrawn the troops. My decision to attack at this time and place was based on the best information available. The troops, the air, and the Navy did all that

bravery and devotion to duty could do. If any blame
or fault attaches to the attempt it is mine alone.[2]

The speech was never given due to the success of the operation. However, it shows the importance and weight that is carried with decision-making. Leaders throughout history have relied on this thought process to make the most well-informed decisions. In the face of fear, we walk with confidence yet unable to control outcomes. But that lack of control should not stop us from making decisions.

## OWN YOUR DECISIONS

The good. The bad. The indecisive. The good is when you own your decision and live with the outcome. The bad is when you make the decision, but instead of owning it, you play the blame game: "It's not my fault!" Indecision is the worst, because in pursuing impossible perfection, you become paralyzed. Here's a tip: Don't apply for a job that oversees others if you fear making decisions or want everything to be perfect. Nothing is more frustrating than indecisive leaders who won't own their decisions.

My two-year-old son was straddling the threshold of our back door while I stood there propping it open. I said, "In or out? Make a decision." I wanted to know what he was planning because his decision would affect whether I stayed inside or went outside. This incident reminded me of a much deeper revelation. Our decisions affect not only ourselves; they affect everyone around us. Transitioning from a thought to a decision changes everything. It creates a ripple effect that sets off a series of events. By owning your thoughts, you are opening yourself to potential conflict. And the more conflict, the more meaningful the decisions. Napoleon Bonaparte said, "Nothing is more difficult, and therefore more precious, than to be able to decide." Making decisions is one of the most difficult yet rewarding things people can do. Every journey requires decisions. So here's a question for you: Are you in or out? It's time to decide. And when you do, own it.

## SPEAK YOUR DECISIONS

At some point you must give voice to your decisions. The more important the decision the less trivial words become. An offhand comment can have a devastating impact on someone looking for your guidance and approval; in the same breath, an offhand comment can bring encouragement and inspiration. That's why I'm very careful with words, a lesson which, unfortunately, I learned the hard way.

When I first became pastor, I was somewhat of a loose cannon with words. If I had an opinion, I'd state it; that is, until one day someone re-quoted me and I said, "I didn't say that, did I?" To which they recited when and where. It was embarrassing. I made up my mind then and there I would be more careful with my words.

Whether spoken or written, words impact our lives every day. They possess the unique power to do many things, like start wars or build bridges. Words can be as cold and sharp as an icicle or as hot and sweet as hot chocolate on a cold winter day. Words are important. How you frame and speak your decisions matters. You can have the best idea in the world, but if you don't frame or communicate it properly, it isn't going anywhere. Why? Because you'll need others to get on board with it—which they won't do if they're offended.

## CONNECTING OTHERS TO YOUR DECISION

Once you launch your thoughts into the stratosphere, you will be held responsible for them. If you speak your thoughts and decisions in today's world, you're taking a major risk. You have to manage your expectations. I know a lot of good salesmen who don't follow things through. Before you make a decision, count the cost and follow through.

As my toddler stood in the doorway with one foot in and one foot out, I let him make the inside-or-outside decision, knowing it would affect mine. Our decisions affect others. When we make a decision, it's wonderful when others agree with us. There will be harmony and synergy. However, many times our decisions meet resistance, hostility, stress, anxiety, or even loss of relationship. I'd like to introduce you to five types of people who will have negative opinions about your decisions and how they most likely will respond.

1. The Warrior stays on the warpath. The theme song of his life is "We're not gonna take it! No, we're not gonna take it!"

2. The Victim lives in woe-is-me land. She is constantly waiting for someone to save her.

3. The Denier slips into a pleasant state of denial. "I'm OK, you're OK, everything is OK!"

4. The Cynic sits back to see what will happen. Every sentence begins with, "I don't think it'll work, but we'll just see."

5. The Ignorer disregards reality and always believes every situation will just take care of itself.

No matter what approach is taken, natural consequences will follow. The Warrior will fight your decisions. The Victim will turn your decision around; it will become all about them. The Denier will be crushed by reality. The Cynic will contribute nothing except a cloud of doubt. When things don't take care of themselves, the Ignorer will crawl into a hole. These traits are obviously negative, but they are always going to be there.

You have to answer the question, "What's more important: their response or my decision?"

Then there are the positive-response people:

1. The Mentor's chief aim is to develop your potential.

2. The Encourager inspires you to be great and brings out your best.

3. The Confronter's encounters are built on trust, timing, and tears. "Faithful are the wounds of a friend; but the kisses of an enemy are deceitful" (Proverbs 27:6).

4. The Intercessor is a connector. She takes bold actions, is humble in her relationships, and builds bridges.

5. The Partner is Batman's sidekick, Robin, and the Lone Ranger's riding partner, Tonto. He helps to bear the load.

All ten of these voices, both negative and positive, will be heard at some point in your life. How you connect them to your dream is up to you. With positive voices, it's important to listen, learn, and apply because they may have traveled the path before you and their thoughts matter. So ask crucial questions, put into effect what you are learning, and don't forget to show gratitude. Have you seen the inspirational poster of the turtle on the fence post? You know it didn't get there on its own.

We are so thoroughly immersed in a rapidly evolving world via texting, email, and social media that we often forget the most powerful tool we have is our ability to develop relationships. Life is about connecting, not just communicating. Your dream will evaporate if you don't connect others to it. Get on the same side of the table with the people you're working with and start forming connections. A relational approach (rather than a clinical transactional approach) builds bridges of communication that will lead not only to the successful realization of your dream, but it also will pave the way back to the table with them in the future.

## THREE BIG IDEAS

1. When you make a decision, whether good, bad, or indifferent, you have to own it.

2. Life is full of decisions. Although you stand at the crossroads craning your neck to see as far as you can see, you hesitate to make those decisions because the outcome is uncertain. You can either be prudent and attempt to make the best decision with the information available, or you can become paralyzed by fear and indecision. The step between prudence and fear is short and steep.

3. There are ten characters you will connect with along the way:

    a) The Warrior stays on the warpath. His theme song is "We're not gonna take it! No, we're not gonna take it!"

    b) The Victim lives in woe-is-me land. She is constantly waiting for someone to save her.

    c) The Denier slips into a pleasant state of denial. "I'm OK. You're OK. Everything is OK!"

    d) The Cynic sits back to see what happens. Every sentence begins with, "I don't think it'll work. We'll just have to wait and see."

e) The Ignorer disregards reality and believes every situation will just take care of itself.

f) The Mentor's chief aim is to develop your potential.

g) The Encourager inspires you to be great and brings out your best.

h) The Confronter's encounters are built on trust, timing, and tears. "Faithful are the wounds of a friend, but the kisses of an enemy are deceitful" (Proverbs 27:6).

i) The Intercessor is a connector. She takes bold actions, is humble in her relationships, and builds bridges.

j) The Partner is Batman's sidekick, Robin, and the Lone Ranger's riding partner, Tonto. He helps to bear the load.

## THREE BIG QUESTIONS

1.  What is your in/out decision?

    _____

    _____

2.  Write your elevator speech: two or three sentences that encapsulate the problem, state the facts, and reveal the decision.

    _____

    _____

3.  Life is about connecting, not just communicating. List the names of your

    Mentor  _____

    Encourager  _____

    Confronter  _____

    Intercessor  _____

    Partner  _____

# BELIEVE THE GOOD

*"Burn the ships, cut the ties." –For King & Country*

A young couple in their twenties decided to have professional pictures taken. They went to the photoshoot and had a good time posing. They were so in love. A few days passed and the photographer called the girl to come pick up the photos. While there, she asked for a duplicate copy of her favorite picture. She wanted to give it to her boyfriend as a gift. She wrote the following on the back: *"My dearest Tom, I love you with all my heart. I love you more and more each day. I will love you forever and ever. I am yours for all eternity. Signed, Dianne. P.S. If we ever break up, I want this picture back."* It's funny, but true. We see pictures of "great relationships" on social media, and we think those are goals that we want in our lives. We don't see the commitment and belief in each other it took to get to that point.

Before we go any further, I have a question for you: Do you believe in what you're doing? I'm asking because your willingness to embody your decision to the point of belief has a direct correlation to the credibility of your decision. Becoming one with your decision changes everything. When it becomes clear to those around you that you have personally embraced the dream, it's like giving them permission to do the same. At this point, the dream becomes a tangible belief.

Jesus told a parable about two men who were out in the field guarding the owner's sheep when a wolf attacked the flock. The man who stood his ground and fought off the wolf was labeled a shepherd; the man who ran at the sight of the wolf was labeled a hireling. The shepherd acted for the cause; the hireling acted for his own benefit. Once the benefit or security was gone, so was the man. Your beliefs are revealed when the wolf charges into the field. You can convince yourself that you believe in your thoughts and decisions, but until you come face to face with action, you and everyone else discover what you really believe. So I ask again, "Do you believe in what you're doing?"

In 1983, my parents made the decision to say, "I do." Thirty-seven years later, they still "do." Their journey hasn't been easy. It's been through sickness and health, good times and bad times. My dad has worked two jobs my entire life. I've seen my parents go the extra mile for me and my brother. They lived their lives for others. Their decision was greater than their own benefit or security. They believed in their decisions.

Belief is always tested. It's one thing to talk about your dreams and beliefs; it's another to do something about them. The only real measure of belief is action. There are usually four responses: (1) cop-outs: people who have no goals and do not commit; (2) hold-outs: people who don't know if they can reach their goals, so they're afraid to commit; (3) drop-outs: people who start but quit when the going gets tough; (4) sold-outs: people who set goals, commit to them, and pay the price to reach them.

## BELIEF: BURN THE SHIPS

Legend has it that on April 21, 1519, the Spanish explorer Hernando Cortez sailed into the harbor of Vera Cruz, Mexico, with his six hundred men. Over the next two years his vastly outnumbered forces defeated Montezuma and all the warriors of the Aztec Empire, making Cortez the conqueror of Mexico. Two prior expeditions had failed to establish a colony on Mexican soil, so how did Cortez accomplish this victory? He knew from the beginning that he and his men faced incredible odds. He knew the road before them would be dangerous and difficult. He knew his men would be tempted to abandon their quest and return to Spain. So, as soon as Cortez and his men came ashore and unloaded their provisions, he ordered their entire fleet of eleven ships to be burned. His men stood on the shore and watched as their only possibility of retreat burned and sank. They knew beyond any doubt there was no return, no turning back. Their only option was to conquer or die. They believed in what they were doing. *Do you believe in what you're doing?*

## BELIEF: 185 VERSUS 1,800

I have a medal hanging in my office stating I finished the Rock n Roll Half Marathon in San Antonio, Texas. The course skirted one of the most visited tourist attractions in San Antonio—the Alamo, a Spanish mission from the 1800s. It's a popular attraction due to a thirteen-day battle in 1836 between 1,800 Mexican troops led by Santa Anna and 185 Texans led by William Travis. On February 23, the Mexican army marched into San Antonio to retake Texas. On March 6, after two repelled attacks, the Mexican soldiers scaled the walls of the Alamo, pushing the Texans into the inner walls of the mission. There was no escape. Once the battle was concluded, 400–600 of the Mexican Republic soldiers lay either killed or wounded, and all 185 Texans were dead. But here's the interesting thing to me: the Texans knew they were outnumbered. They knew they were trapped within the walls of the Alamo. They knew that due to the American-Mexican treaty they would receive no help from the US government, for Texas was its own Republic. So why did they stay? Why not retreat when they had the chance? The answer comes in the form of a story passed down through history. The inscription on a plaque at the Alamo says this:

> Legend states that in 1836 Lt. Col. William Barret Travis unsheathed his sword and drew a line on this ground before his battle-weary men stating, "Those prepared to give their lives in freedom's cause come over to me!"

All 185 Texans crossed the line because they believed in what they were doing. When you get to the point in your dream where the line is drawn, will you believe in what you're doing?

## ALL IN

What fills your heart and makes you sing? What opens the tear ducts of compassion and breaks your heart? What dream lifts your spirit? What dream makes you believe there is something more out there? What decisions are you are willing to make that are beyond your current reality? Are you all in?

If you feel as if you can no longer hold back the adrenalin that is pumping through your veins, then your response must be like Nike's: "Just do it!" Think about it. You have dreamed the greatest dream of your life, you know exactly what you want, you know the time you've already invested and the time it will take in the future. You're focused and have done your homework. You've communicated with those who have gone before you. The plan in your head and hand is solid. You trust the people with whom you've surrounded yourself. It's time to move forward.

Perhaps some inspiration from the pen of Dr. Seuss would be appropriate. Here are the words from the last pages of his book, *Oh the Places You'll Go!*

> *And will you succeed? YES! You will, indeed!*
> *(98 and ¾ percent guaranteed.)*
> *KID, YOU'LL MOVE MOUTAINS!*
> *So...*
> *Be your name Buxbaum or Bixby or Bray*
> *Or Mordecai Ali Van Allen O'Shae,*
> *You're off to Great Places!*
> *Today is your day!*
> *Your mountain is waiting!*
> *So... get on your way!*

## THREE BIG IDEAS

1. Your beliefs are revealed when the wolf charges into the field. You can convince yourself that you believe in your thoughts and decisions—until you come face to face with action.

2. When it becomes your belief, there are usually four types of responses: (1) cop-outs: people who have no goals but do not commit; (2) hold-outs: people who don't know if they can reach their goals, so they're afraid to commit; (3) drop-outs: people who start but quit when the going gets tough; (4) sold-outs: people who set goals, commit to them, and pay the price to reach them.

3. If you feel you no longer can hold back the adrenalin that's pumping in your veins, then your response must be like Nike's: Just do it!

## THREE BIG QUESTIONS

1. Do you believe so strongly in what you're doing that you're willing to burn the ships?

   _____

   _____

2. What does a burned ship look like to you?

   _____

   _____

3. What is the caution you feel in your mind right now?

   _____

   _____

# ACTION—GET IT DONE

*"The most untutored person with passion is more persuasive than the most eloquent without."*
-Francois VI, Duc de la Rochefoucauld

Recently, Ashley and I sat in the church office during my phone conversation with a man who informed me that final approval had been granted to launch a new church in Manhattan. The only thing standing between planning and implementation were a few more signatures on the approval. We had submitted a plan, obtained local leadership, and now were working through steps to secure financial support for the proposed budget. As I hung up the phone, Ashley asked uncertainly, "Are we ready for a second campus?" To which I responded, "This is what we've been preparing for."

How did I know it was time to take the leap? Everything leading up to this point had been focused on preparation and implementation. Now it was time to shift to execution. The ability to produce results has always been the separation line of success. On one side of the line are those who produce results; on the other side are those who have an excuse why they didn't.

Christopher Columbus had just come back from discovering the New World and was sitting in a pub with some buddies. One of them was giving him a hard time, saying, "All you did was get in boat and start sailing. It's ridiculous—you being a national hero for simply riding in a boat. Anyone could have done what you did."

Columbus spotted a hardboiled egg on the bar and handed it to his friend with a challenge: "Let's see if you can stand this egg on end." The man tried, but the egg constantly rolled back down on its side. He handed it back to Columbus, saying, "Your turn." Columbus picked up the egg and smashed the bottom of it into the table. The egg sat smugly upright. The man snapped, "I could have done that!" To which Columbus said, "But you didn't."

Anyone can have an idea, but what you do with the idea is the point of separation.

## PRODUCTION MATTERS

Five frogs were sitting on a log. Four decided to jump off. How many were left? Answer: five. Why? Because there's a difference between deciding to do something and actually doing it. Those who deliver results live on their performance, not their potential. Poet Walt Mason wrote a poem called "The Welcome Man." Here is a portion of that poem:

*There is a man in this world who is never turned*
> *down,*
*Whenever he chances to stray;*
*He gets the glad hand in the populous town,*
> *Or out where the farmers make hay;*
*He is greeted with pleasure on deserts of sand,*
> *And deep in the isles of the woods;*
*Wherever he goes there's the welcoming hand –*
> *He's the man who delivers the good.*[1]

Regardless of odds, obstacles, or circumstances, our actions must produce. If we don't produce, then we won't thrive. You might be wondering, *Well, you're a pastor. Why are you focused on production?* Jesus taught production as a principle of His kingdom, and it most definitely correlates to life in general. This principle is found in Jesus' Parable of the Fig Tree:

> A man had a fig tree. He planted it in his garden. He came looking for some fruit on it, but he found none. He had a servant who took care of his garden. So he said to his servant, "I have been looking for fruit on this tree for three years, but I never find any. Cut it down! Why should it waste the ground?" But the servant answered, "Master, let the tree have one more year to produce fruit. Let me dig up the dirt around it and fertilize it. Maybe the tree will have fruit on it next year. If it still does not produce, then you can cut it down." (Luke 13:6–9, ERV)

We were created to be productive. Cal Newport, in his book *Deep Work*, posits this formula for high-quality work produced:

High-Quality Work Produced = (Time Spent) x (Intensity of Focus)

I would add one more element to the equation: Trust Earned.

## TIME SPENT

Did you know the world has a Domino Day? No? I didn't either. On November 13, 2009, a domino company coordinated an event called "The World in Domino—The Show with the Flow," during which a single domino set in motion the fall of 4,491,863 dominoes that unleashed more than 94,000 joules of energy. To put that in perspective, that's the amount of energy it would take for you to do around 545 pushups. Each domino represents a miniscule amount of energy, but the more dominos in line the more potential energy is created. Line up enough and, with a simple flick, you can start a chain reaction of surprising power. I've done this with my kids many times, though on a much smaller scale. But whether 10 or 4,491,863 dominos, this phenomenon reveals this truth: success is sequential, not simultaneous. I call it the domino effect.

Productivity works the same way: line up your priorities first, then your essentials, then your extras, and refuse to stop until the tasks are accomplished. Do the first right thing, then the second right thing, and so on. Over time, it adds up and incredible power is unleashed. From each individual increment to the finished product, time spent is essential to high-quality productivity.

Experts are full of information in their specific field, but it doesn't happen through osmosis; they study and learn over time. Expertise and super talents are developed little by little, one piano etude at a time, one baseball pitch at a time, one lab experiment at a time. Achieving success takes time.

I remember my first half-marathon, the Rock n Roll Series in Dallas, Texas. At every mile marker there was a band playing music. If you could hear the music, you knew you were close to another mile marker. Thinking about the entire course of 13.1 miles may be overwhelming, but thinking about a mile at a time isn't. You don't think about running the whole marathon; you just run to the next mile marker. Then you keep moving.

We live in a microwave society. If you don't get your fast food in thirty seconds, you want to trash the store. Our generation can't tolerate slowness; we want everything to happen quickly. Think about the last sitcom you watched. To every show there is a beginning, a crisis, and a glorious conclusion in which everyone lives happily ever after—all in less than thirty minutes. But meaningful growth and productivity move sequentially and incrementally. In real life, this takes time.

## INTENSITY OF FOCUS

"A journey of a thousand miles begins with a single step." That might be a worn-out cliché, but it's packs a lot of wisdom. Too many people abandon the journey after the first step is taken. How do you stay motived to keep pressing toward your goal? It requires consistent focus on your core and purpose. Don't focus on being busy; focus on being productive. Pay the most attention to what matters most.

Psychological researcher Carol Dweck and her collaborators discovered how an incremental change can make a massive difference. In a TEDx talk, Dweck said,

> I heard about a high school in Chicago where students had to pass a certain number of courses to graduate, and if they didn't pass a course, they got the grade "NOT YET." And I thought that was fantastic, because if you get a failing grade, you think, I'm nothing, I'm nowhere. But if you get the grade "Not Yet" you understand that you're on a learning curve. It gives you a path to the future."[2]

Dweck's research showed how the high school principal fostered a culture of focusing on the process rather than the end result.

Earlier in this book I referenced a winning mindset and highlighted Coach Nick Saban, who derived his winning philosophy from Dr. Lionel Rosen, a Michigan State University psychiatry professor. Rosen taught the Michigan State Spartans a form of step-by-step thinking: "The average play in a football game last[s] seven seconds. The players would concentrate only on winning those seconds, take a rest between plays, then do it all over again. There would be no focus at all on the scoreboard or the end results."[3] Just concentrate on finishing the small task in front of you.

## TRUST EARNED

If you don't put in the time, you won't produce. If you don't produce, your dreams will never come true. It doesn't matter how skilled or talented you are, it takes time and focus to get results. Results breed trust. When people see that you can produce and they buy in to your dream, it changes the dynamics of the relationship and organization. Trust is not given automatically.

In the 1860s, there was a famous French tightrope walker named Charles Blondin. One of his most daring feats was to walk a tightrope stretched 1,100 feet (over a quarter mile) across Niagara Gorge. The rope was sixteen feet above the falls. He had crossed it numerous times and crowds began to gather to watch his daring feats. He got creative and started pushing a wheelbarrow along the tightrope. One day after a crossing, he asked a young boy, "Do you believe I could push a person in the wheelbarrow across the falls?" The boy exclaimed enthusiastically, "Yes sir, I really do!" To which Blondin replied, "Well then, get in." I don't know if the boy got in or not, but I'm sure it made him evaluate his level of trust.

Trust is a rare commodity in our world. One of the most obvious societal changes I've seen in my lifetime has to do with the matter of trust. We live in a world that constantly faces the question "Should I trust?" Trust casts light; distrust casts shadows. Many elements contribute to the question of trust. For instance, a person's natural skepticism may be a result of dealing with bad leaders, partial politics, abusive childhoods, or from social media or the news media. A lack of trust, whether justified or not, has produced a jaded, cynical, suspicious generation. It is an epidemic. It is sad because trust is such a necessary ingredient in every aspect of our life.

A lack of trust has cost us in a multitude of ways. We install various security methods—locks, surveillance, extra lighting, guard services, and the like—because we don't know if others will try to steal our property or do us physical harm. In some places, people are afraid to call the police, because they think the police might harm them. Observe the difference in our world since 9/11. The cost of security worldwide has been astronomical. Everyone is looked at with suspicion. Instead of getting to the airport thirty minutes early for a flight, we now are told to get there ninety minutes early to allow for security procedures.

It's a rare and precious thing to find someone we can trust. Trust is receiving the quiet assurance that persuades us, that gives us confidence, that assures us, and helps us yield to ways we don't understand or don't like or when everything doesn't go our way. Every day is not a zip-a-dee-do-dah day. Some days are dark, scary, disappointing. That's when trust comes into play. Trust involves closeness or intimacy.

Healthy relationships are built upon and maintained by trust. Trust is the highest expression of faith. It is much more than belief, and it is more than confidence in what God can do. It is a firm belief or confidence in the honesty, integrity, reliability, or justice of another person or thing. It comes from closeness and intimacy. Sometimes your trust is betrayed. Sometimes you betray others who trust you. It's inevitable. Despite our best intentions, we will fall short in both categories. But it is better to trust and be trusted than to have never trusted at all. Refuse to allow your heart to become hard. It's all right to trust again.

Here's a suggestion: give yourself permission to trust others, to believe the best in others, and that others are worth trusting. It's a miserable life thinking that everyone is "out to get you." Make up in your mind that they aren't out to get you, because most often they're not.

## TRUST YOUR CALL

As I said in chapter 2, I felt our move to New York was a calling, and I was passionate about it. If you're going to take the leap, burn the ship, or draw the line in the sand, then be passionate about it! Francois VI, Duc de La Rochefoucauld, said, "The most untutored person with passion is more persuasive than the most eloquent without." If you're not ready to shout to the world what you're doing, don't do it!

I remember telling my college instructor that I was called to plant a church in New York City. Over ten years later I still remember his response: "Come back in ten years and I'll believe you." It was a challenge. The calling always needs a challenge to offer you the edge. And now, well over ten years later, the passion still lives. Before you act, make sure the passion is still thrumming through every fiber of your being.

## TRUST YOUR TRAINING

Training is a big deal. We should do everything in our power to be prepared for what comes our way. "A big confidence builder in doing a negotiation is preparation. The more prepared you are, the less nervous and more effective you will be. You won't be busy trying to remember what you're supposed to do next. You won't be as worried about what you don't know."[4]

A helicopter pilot who flew from an aircraft carrier in the Pacific told this story:

> I was flying the helicopter back to the ship when a blinding fog rolled in. Flying at a low altitude, I knew that a single mistake would plunge my crew and me into the ocean. Worse yet, I was experiencing a complete loss of balance—which is common for pilots flying by instruments. This loss of balance—known as vertigo—was so bad that despite the instrument readings I was certain that I was lying on my side. For fifteen minutes I flew the helicopter by its instruments, fighting the urge to turn it according to my feeling. When we finally broke safely through the fog, I was deeply thankful I had been trained to rely upon my instruments rather than on my feelings.[5]

That is what people who live by trust do; they remember that feelings can be misleading, but truth is reliable, trustworthy, and consistent. The pilot was trained to trust his instruments. His training did not happen overnight; it was built over time. And he had to trust it, even in the fog.

## THE HOUSE OF PRODUCTIVITY

Think of it as a three-story house. *The ground floor is time.* Everyone has the same twenty-four hours in a day. Success is sequential, not instant or simultaneous. The secret is to keep moving forward.

*The second floor is focus.* This is where you believe in the plan and also in yourself. You're competent enough to start small. One of the main failures people experience is when it's time to launch, they want to launch big. But the hare didn't win; the tortoise did. The mighty oak was once a tiny acorn. The big train was once the little engine that could. Give yourself permission to start small. It doesn't mean you have a small vision; it means you are taking an appropriate first step. A motivational speaker said it's better to have small dreams and big work ethics. Believe in what you're doing even if it seems small. Eventually, over time, you will produce. Stay focused.

*The third floor is trust.* This is like the dark attic. It's a nerve-wracking place to be because you have to trust what you know rather than what you can see. You have to trust your calling and training rather than your eyesight. Generating that trust is hard work; it's even harder to maintain it. Not many achieve it, but when you do, it changes everything.

## LET'S GET IT DONE!

I was standing on a makeshift ledge twenty to thirty feet in the air, gripping a knot at the end of a rope. Below, approximately five yards of land stretched between me and the river. Heart pounding, I said to myself, "OK, Donny, don't be a chicken and climb back down. You know you have to do this. Take a deep breath, and *just do it.*" I can still replay the moment when I decided to launch myself into the air and let go of the rope. Even now, I feel myself back on that ledge, breathing deep with the decisions I have to make. I ask myself, "Am I competent enough to commit and get it done?"

In the Gospel of Luke, Jesus shared two stories about getting things done. The first story was of a man who had to abandon his building project because he ran out of funds. He laid a foundation but couldn't finish the tower and was mocked for his lack of planning and preparation. The second story was of a king who was planning to engage in battle. He looked at the enemy's twenty-thousand-man force, then at his own one thousand men.

He thinks, *I refuse to take such a foolhardy risk with the lives of my men. I'm going to send a delegation to the enemy to negotiate peace.* Calculating this way is not a lack of faith, but foresight based on insight and hindsight.

*A Note from Ashley:*

*"Deeper" defined means extending far down from the top or surface. Reading that definition automatically makes me tense up because it makes me think of deep water. I have an intense fear of deep water because I can't swim. Right after we got married, Donny decided he was going to teach me how to swim. The short story is I still don't know how to swim. I almost drowned my new husband in the shallow end of the pool!*

*The shore or the shallow end of the pool is my favorite, because my feet are touching the ground and I'm still in control. I'm not all the way in the water; my face is above the surface. I can easily get to lakeshore or climb out of the pool.*

*Even though I don't know how to swim, I did spend a lot time around a pool with some of my college friends, mainly because I dog-sat for a family that had an amazing pool. There were always plenty of girls willing to "help" me watch the poodle. I began to notice there were three types of girls who came to swim: (1) The girls who were worried about getting their hair wet. They were ones I usually ended up spending the day with on the shallow end. (2) The girls who came for the socializing. They weren't really committed to spending the day swimming. It didn't matter if they were in or out the pool because they didn't really have anything invested. (3) The girls, like my roommate, who would do a cannonball off the diving board first thing. She stayed in the pool for hours. Her hair was wet; she was in the deep water; she was investing her day in that pool. I was often jealous of how much she enjoyed the water. Because of her, I wanted to learn to swim. I quickly realized that while the shallow end can be nice and safe, the ones who are willing to take the dive into the deeper waters are the ones who get the most benefit and enjoyment out of the water.*

## THREE BIG IDEAS

1. American Civil Rights leader Whitney M. Young Jr. said, "It is better to be prepared for an opportunity and not get one than to have an opportunity and not be prepared."

2. You have dreamed the greatest dream of your life, you know exactly what you want, you've done the homework, and you've communicated with those who have gone before you. The plan in your head and hand is solid. You trust the people with whom you've surrounded yourself. Let's get it done!

3. While the shallow end can be nice and safe, the ones who are willing to dive into deeper waters are the ones who get the most benefit and enjoyment out of the water.

## THREE BIG QUESTIONS

1. How much time do you spend on what you want the most?

   _____

   _____

2. What do you need to eliminate from your life in order to focus?

   _____

   _____

3. List the names of the people you trust.

   _____

   _____

# WHEN REALITY STRIKES

*"That's so 2020." –Everyone in 2020*

## WELCOME TO REALITY

During the final months of 2019, I wrote a booklet called *The 2020 Game Plan*. It was an internal document for our church leadership team highlighting vision, goals, and direction of the upcoming year. Then on December 1, 2019, we had a leadership meeting to discuss the plan. It was a great meeting. We began by sharing the wins of 2019 and what we intended to do moving forward. The air was electric with excitement and times were good.

But then, toward the end of the first quarter, we were blindsided by COVID-19, a pandemic we were told would likely spread to the United States in January 2020. News came trickling in about people dying in China and Italy and elsewhere, but as the weeks drifted by, few people were paying attention to the imminent threat to our own nation. Then on March 15 we had to shut down in-person church services and the entire nation was in lockdown. Everything began moving so fast that I forgot about the game plan; that is, until I was on a staff call and my assistant asked, "How's the game plan working out?" We laughed and I responded, "It's in the bottom of my desk drawer collecting dust alongside all of the other irrelevant documents I can't seem to muster the gumption to throw out."

These experiences brought me to a revelation and a question: What do you do when you've thought, decided, believed, and acted, and then reality drops a bomb and changes everything? What do you do when all of your plans are voided? What do you do when everything you've envisioned disappears? What do you do when your vision doesn't resemble the reality? In this chapter we will explore different stories and models of dealing with change and transition in our lives.

## HALFTIME ADJUSTMENTS

Everyone has had a crisis, and we will continue to have crises. Hardships are a part of life. A crisis is when you have more coming at you than you can handle, from one direction—or many directions at once. A crisis is when you're facing an adversary you know you can't conquer or a situation you can't control.

How you view and respond to those crises will make all the difference. The actions you take during the crisis will determine the outcome. A crisis can be the best thing that happens to you or the worst thing that happens to you, depending on your response. You may have heard the phrase "Never waste a good crisis." Some attribute it to politicians, but the phrase actually was found in a 2009 report evaluating the British construction industry's performance. The author of the report summarized recommendations that, if adopted, would transform the Great Recession into an opportunity to correct their performance. The idea was to use the crisis to find a new and improved direction. The author understood that the way they dealt with a crisis would determine their future.

Change is constant—the move to a new home, the retirement of the company founder, the reorganization of the roles on the team, and so on. Transition, on the other hand, is psychological. Transition consultant William Bridges developed a three-phase process to help people deal with transition:

1. Ending, Losing, and Letting Go—helps people deal with their tangible and intangible losses and mentally prepare to move on.

2. Neutral Zone—the loss of purpose experienced by people who have tied their identity to the pursuits of their old life. It's a place of both risk and opportunity, based upon how it is handled.

3. New Beginning—where people begin to develop new experiences. William Bridges distinguishes between "starts" and "beginnings": a start occurs when people begin building new skills and achieve a few small successes; a beginning occurs when, through psychological and behavioral changes, a person assumes a new behavioral identity.

This type of transition plays out on many fronts in people's lives: new parents who must let go of their old lives and embrace a new family structure; marriages that have ended in divorce; death of a loved one that results in pain and physiological anguish. There is a clear and understandable path that, if followed, can guide an individual from their old life to a new beginning.

Jim Lovell was leading the Apollo 13 mission to the moon when the Saturn rocket that was powering them into orbit malfunctioned. Two days into the flight, the number-two oxygen tank blew up, causing the number-one tank to also fail. The command module's normal supply of electricity, light, and water was lost, and they were two hundred thousand miles from earth. With no heat, temperatures dropped to thirty-eight degrees. They had to ration water to six ounces per day.

Lovell calculated that their chances of survival were slim, but he, along with mission control, threw those thoughts out and instead concentrated on figuring out how to get the crew home safely. Unbelievably, flight controllers were able to write new procedures in only three days—instead of the usual three months. In the end, the crew splashed down safely in the Pacific Ocean after six days in space. In the aftermath, Apollo 13 was classified as a "successful failure" because they invented new ways of rescuing the crews of aborted missions.

There's a difference between reluctantly conceding that change is inevitable and believing it is essential to growth and success. Sometimes change is forced upon you; other times the transition is undertaken intentionally. People who are reluctant to change resign themselves to reactive thinking; those who see change as essential and proactive make it work for them. We cannot grow without change. A better today means that something improved yesterday. We should constantly be adjusting and shifting.

## REALITY SHIFT

As a Louisiana kid, I loved the fact that at one point, our state was the largest. That was in 1803 when Thomas Jefferson negotiated the Louisiana Purchase. But what good is that big land mass if you're not going to explore it? So Jefferson wrote a letter to his good friend Meriwether Lewis and asked him not only to explore this new frontier but to find a water passage from the Mississippi River to the Pacific Ocean, which would benefit the nation's trade and travel. Simple right? All they had to do was hire the best team and start canoeing up the river. Lewis accepted the request of his president and enlisted the help of his good friend and co-commander, William Clark. They took off with a keelboat and two canoes beneath them, paddles in hand, and a vision of the passage in front of them.

They paddled up the Missouri River against the current, expecting to find an easy waterway across the continent. But more than a year into the expedition, they hit a snag at the headwaters of the Missouri River in what is now southwest Montana. Reality set in when the river petered out and they came face to face with the Rocky Mountains. At this point they had two options: (1) They could turn around and go back, telling the president they had given it their best shot. (2) They could attempt to find another water route. What should they do? What would you do? They had to face the fact that their assumptions about the western terrain being the same as the eastern terrain were wrong. Their journey was put on hold.

Which brings me to a small side note. Never assume anything. Next time you're in a conversation, ask for clarity: "Do you mind defining that for me?" "I don't' quite understand what you're saying—can you simplify it?" or simply "Meaning?" If you're on the receiving end to one of these questions, it's your turn to be clear and concise. There's something within each of us that responds in appreciation when things are made clear.

Lewis and Clark were at the point of decision. What could they do when their crew had been trained to ride the riverways and now they were staring at the formidable Rocky Mountains? A member of the corps later recorded his response, saying they "proceeded over the most terrible mountains I ever beheld."[4] Crossing the Continental Divide was bad enough, but after that came the most dangerous leg of the journey: crossing the Bitterroot Mountains. They slogged eleven days through deep snow in mid-September.

But the effort paid off. On the other side of the mountains they connected with Idaho's Clearwater River and were gratified to find they now were paddling with the current. They followed the Snake River, then entered the great Columbia River, receiving their first view of the Pacific Ocean on November 1, 1805.

When we came face to face with the COVID-19 virus, we felt stranded. Our right to gather for corporate worship was taken away. Our weekly connect groups were canceled. Our great plans for Easter events fell by the wayside. Everything in the game plan was now irrelevant. We were living in a world for which we were totally unprepared . . . or so we thought.

In today's world information changes so quickly that what is relevant today may not be relevant tomorrow. Many attempt to handle disappointments with fear, resentment, and bitterness. But disappointments and setbacks are an inevitable part of life. What really matters is how we respond—when someone else gets the promotion, when the team makes a decision we disagree with, when our previous reality is no longer valid. When the expedition's canoes were no longer useful, they came to the conclusion that going backward was not an option. They traded the canoes for mountain boots. The "river rats" became "mountain climbers."

## REMAIN FOCUSED ON THE OBJECTIVE

When reality strikes, remember your purpose. David, who would later become the second king of the nation of Israel, stood before King Saul and said, "Is there not a cause?" Saul and his men were cowering in fear because of the threats of a Philistine giant. Saul looked at David, who, as a teenager, was raring to face up to the giant. He clearly didn't think David had a chance. He offered his personal armor to David, but the boy rejected it because he had never tried it before. Armed only with his shepherd's sling and five smooth stones, he ran to face the great giant. He wasn't focused on possible failure—he was focused on championing a cause.

During our first staff meeting of the COVID-19 era, we began developing a new strategy. Instead of a sanctuary-based church, we shifted to a public square type church, realizing that the "public square" was now online. We began streaming our services. Our ministry departments conducted weekly video chats where people could connect with one another. In a sense, this change strengthened our church community.

Adversity has a way of bringing people together. But there is peril in attempting a new strategy: no one has tried it before. You have your vision and your map, but you can't see what's on the other side of the mountains. Vision must shift to seeing yourself as you really are and being able to define reality in your present state. It's holding on to what matters and letting go of everything else. A new strategy demands a new mindset.

The purpose of Westchester Church has not changed. It has always been giving people hope and bringing them spiritual and relational connection. That is our Pacific Ocean. We had built some nice canoes to get us there, but those canoes were now irrelevant. To get where we had never been before, we had three options: (1) become frustrated over the irrelevancy of our previous map and abort the mission, (2) continue doing the same things we had been doing—like attempting to cross the mountains in our canoes, or (3) march off the map into the unknown.

We chose to march off the map. We then had to figure out what that looked like. I called a meeting with our church leaders and shared with them a vision for the future. Our objectives remained steadfast; we still wanted to bring hope and keep every-one connected. But we had to acknowledge we couldn't achieve those objectives using the same old modus operandi. We devised a new strategy for moving forward and filled in the details for what it would look like. At the end of the meeting everyone was ready to put on their climbing shoes, scale the mountains, and face the new territory together. We invested in equipment and went online. Then, when the door opened to resume in-house services, we made another shift. Due to our renting a facility and other factors, we scheduled our services on Saturday at 10:00 AM rather than Sunday. That was totally out of the norm for us, but we had to march off the map to make it work.

There is no "old normal" or "new normal"; instead, nothing is normal. And attempting to create a "new normal" is pointless because everything is constantly shifting. When we were online, some weeks went well, other weeks were total disaster. But we kept going. Courage is the still small voice inside that says, "That bombed, but I'll try again tomorrow." Life is ten percent what happens to you and ninety percent how you respond. Try again. Keep marching forward.

## DEVELOP FROM THE NEGATIVES

I can vividly remember as a child going to the store with my mom to get film developed. Obviously, this was before cell phones with cameras or even before digital cameras. Here's what the developing process used to be. (1) Mom would take the roll of film out of her camera and drop it in a provided bag. (2) She would fill in her info on the bag and drop off the film at the store. (3) The store would have the film developed. (4) A few days later the store would call Mom to let her know the pictures were ready for pick-up. (5) When she picked up the film, they would always ask, "Would you like to keep the negatives?" It didn't hit me till later in life, but I discovered this truth: Life and change are like photography; we develop from the negatives.

Unknown changes are a natural part of life. Failures are going to happen. But the truth is no one reacts to failure in the same way. When some fail, that failure takes over their life, their emotions, and their relationships. They find it hard to move on, especially if they've put a lot of work, energy, and time into whatever they were working on. Others may take failure in stride and overcome it. What's the difference? Why do some people seem to get beyond their failures, but others don't?

Thomas Edison had thousands of failed attempts while trying to invent the lightbulb, but when he finally did complete the project, he shrugged and said he failed his way to success. Another favorite example is Abraham Lincoln, one of the most "successful failures" in American political history. Look at his record: In 1831, at age twenty-three, he attempted to become successful in business, but failed. In 1832, he ran for a legislature post and lost. In 1833, he failed at business again. In 1838 and 1840, he was defeated for speaker. In 1843 and 1848, he was defeated for Congress. In 1855, he was defeated for a Senate post. In 1856, he was defeated for vice president. In 1858, he was defeated for the Senate again. But in 1860, he became the sixteenth president of the United States.

What made the difference? These men had the ability to reframe their failure not as a down-and-out experience but rather as a road to being better next time. When someone spoke of failure to Abraham Lincoln, he would say, "Yes, and let me tell you what I learned from that experience that made me better." Life will provide times of great triumphs and times of great failure, but all of them will be times of great learning. Everyone has setbacks, but at the end of those setbacks, press the re-set button and try again.

## NOT EVERYONE WILL ACCEPT THE NEW REALITY

Do a dictionary search on the word *pruning* and you'll find "a function of cutting away to reduce the extent or reach of something by taking away unwanted or superfluous parts." I don't have a green thumb, but I do know a little about gardening. The flower bed in our yard has a rose bush. A healthy rose bush is vibrant and beautiful, but it won't stay that way without a never-ending process called pruning. Without pruning, a healthy rose bush becomes susceptible to disease and pests, broken branches interfere with healthy new growth, and if left unpruned too long, the rose bush will die. Unfortunately, this happens to some people too—the ones who won't submit to endings (pruning) in order to make room for new beginnings.

Lewis and Clark were standing at the base of the mountains. Weary of the journey, two men decided to revolt. It would have been standard practice to execute them both. However, they were simply demoted from official status and told to leave the expedition. In any change or transition, it is inevitable that some will not make the journey. It simply comes with the territory.

When Jesus veered off the map with His notions of a heavenly kingdom rather than the first century's expected earthly kingdom, Judas, one of His disciples, refused to abandon that perception. He attempted to force Jesus into taking an earthy throne. Jesus expected the betrayal, embraced it, and didn't get offended. Hanging on the cross, He said, "Father forgive them, for they do not know what they do" (Luke 23:34, NKJV). Not everyone will make the journey with you. Accept it, forgive their "betrayal," and keep moving forward.

## REBUILD

Braydon, my oldest son, loves to play with Legos. For his birthday he received a large set of Legos, and it took him three days to build a house, two boats, a dock, and some trees. He was so proud that he accomplished it by himself.

Earlier this week we walked into the bedroom and discovered that Elliot, our youngest, had gotten his hands on the long-labored creations and dismantled all of the pieces. Luckily, Ashley and I saw the destruction before Braydon did and devised the best way to break the news. We told him, "Don't worry. We will deal with Elliot. Everything is still OK because you still have all the pieces, and you still have the instructions. You can have fun rebuilding."

Many people in our world feel broken in health, finance, or relationships. It seems our government and world systems are broken. But I want to offer a word of encouragement: everything that God placed inside of you is still there. You have what it takes to rebuild, so don't give up. Don't let hope die. Keep dreaming and remembering why you do what you do.

Many changes occur in our lives, but the dream is still the main thing. A part of life and achieving the dream is to stay the course through the wins, losses, and lessons. The ability to encourage others, to exude energy and enthusiasm for continuing forward, and to find new ways to communicate the message is paramount to its success.

I asked an elderly pastor who was celebrating his fiftieth church anniversary about his "secret sauce." His response was simple. A grin spread over his face and he said, "We stayed." Different people moved and flowed through the church. Different leaders arose and vanished. But the big picture was always in view. I then asked, "But what was your secret?" He reiterated, "We stayed—through it all." What do you do when reality shows up at your doorstep? You sell the canoes and purchase mountain boots.

## THREE BIG IDEAS

1. What do you do when you've thought, decided, believed, and acted and now reality shows up and changes everything? What do you do when all of your plans are voided? What do you do when everything you've envisioned disappears? What do you do when your vision does not match the reality?

2. William Bridges developed a three-phase model for the process of change:

   a) Ending, Losing, and Letting Go—helps people deal with their tangible and intangible losses and mentally prepares them to move on.

   b) Neutral Zone—the in-between place where one feels a loss of purpose, where people's identities are entangled in their old life. This is a place of both risk and opportunity, based upon how it is handled.

   c) New Beginning—where people begin to develop new experiences. William Bridges distinguishes between "starts" and "beginnings." A start occurs when people start doing new things, and when they start enacting the changes. A beginning occurs when psychological and behavioral changes allow a person to assume a new behavioral identity.

3. Whether you're winning or losing, do it with grace and humility. Everyone has setbacks. Push the re-set button and start climbing.

## THREE BIG QUESTIONS

1. Have you ever been slapped in the face by a wave of reality? Tell your story.

   _____

   _____

2. What strategies did you find that helped you change from a "river rider" to a "mountain climber"?

   _____

   _____

3. What are some of the most important lessons you've learned about change?

   _____

   _____

# Part 3
## A BUTTER TODAY

The next few chapters contain my "butter" story. There's a self-conscience part of me that feels inadequate to write this. Thoughts have flooded my mind, like "Don't get excited; you're still the same old you." I've attempted to suppress the moment and the feelings that came with it: "Is it wise to tell this story? Is it egotistical? After all, I was just a stick of butter in a Thanksgiving Day parade." However, the events I'm going to tell you created a moment of unforgettable awe in my life.

These feelings were resolved as I stood in the back of Studio 1A at the TODAY show, waiting to take my seat at the table for an interview. All I could think was, *I don't deserve to be here.* My mouth was as dry as cotton; it was my first time ever to enter a television studio. I looked around the room and the thought occurred to me, *Who says you don't deserve to be here?* I began encouraging myself: *Just be yourself and give it everything you've got. They wouldn't have asked you to come if you weren't supposed to be here. Be a light. Bring joy. And just be you.*

# Part 3
## A BETTER TODAY

# LITTLE THINGS, BIG THINGS

*"It's always the little things that make the big things happen." –Jeffrey Fry*

Little things are big things. This concept, though easily stated, is not easy to grasp. We tend to believe that in order to have a large impact we need to do something dramatic and big. As a rule, we aren't impressed by small things. We like to go to *big* sales. We don't want to just go to openings, but "grand openings." We don't just want a tall at Starbucks, we want a "Grande." People don't just want to win a million-dollar lottery, they want to win a mega-million lottery. Go Big. But I learned something while snow skiing in Colorado: you can't go on a difficult black diamond trail if first you haven't mastered the easy green circle trail. It's the little things that matter, that bring the magic. It's the extra. Big events have small moments. Like the tiny acorn that grows into a mighty oak, our dreams grow. And there are no small parts.

## CLOWN UNIVERSITY

It was a rainy October Sunday morning and I was wearing my sweatpants and hoodie. I jumped onto the Metro North and headed into the city. Normally I would have jogged from Grand Central to the Lincoln Center, but since it was raining, I took the subway. I found my friend Mallory, who was waiting for me, and we went to the Big Apple Circus. We were there because we had registered at Clown University. That's right—we went to clown school.

Clown University is an event sponsored by Macy's to teach volunteers how to be clowns in their famed Thanksgiving Day Parade. It's an action-packed, high-energy event with over four hundred clowns. We covered a broad range of topics like hydration, energy levels, how to walk, and how to smile. Macy's focuses on clowns because clowns are the heart of the parade. They're the ones who provide the personal touch and keep the excitement levels elevated.

Instructors at Clown U broke us up into groups; Mallory and I were in the breakfast group. Our instructor spent a considerable amount of time talking about the importance of little moments. He said people come to the parade to see *big* things: big balloons, big-name singers, and big floats. But if you've ever been in New York at Thanksgiving time, you'll see the entire city come together for the Macy's parade—from the day-before showcasing the balloons to those who mark off the streets. It's an all-hands-on-deck promotion. Walter Elliot said, "Perseverance is not a long race; it is many short races one after the other." The instructor said, "It's not about the big; *it's about what you do with the little moments that makes the difference.* People will remember the clown that walks up, shakes their hand, and asks, 'Where are you from?' or says, 'Thank you for coming.'" It may be trite, but it's still true: people don't care how much you know until they know how much you care.

During the training event they provided a time slot where you could practice your lines in front of everyone in the center ring. I thought at the time that I was going to be "toast" like toast and butter. So I acted like I was a piece of bread entering into a toaster oven, screaming, "In like bread—out like toast!" The parade typically falls on a cold day, so I practiced the line "Sure is toasty for winter!" It was a crowd pleaser.

Following are a few lessons I learned at Clown U:

## ENERGY

Clown training placed great emphasis on energy level; on a scale of one to ten, one was low energy and ten was high energy. Low energy would be on the fence line; high energy would be in the middle of the street. The subject of energy level was important because the parade route is approximately 2.5 miles long (about five thousand steps), and it takes roughly an hour to get from the starting line to 34th Street. That's eighty-three steps per minute! The instructor said it was best to vary the energy level throughout the parade. I'm afraid I broke that rule; I was pretty much ten from start to end.

In an interview on my YouTube channel, "Better Perspective," health and nutrition specialist Deb Pomeroy spoke on exercise and stress. She said when your body gets enough exercise, it's important not to add any additional stress to it. For example, if you're walking a trail, don't be concerned with how many steps you take . . . just walk. When your body asks you to stop, just stop.

The key is not the number of steps; it's consistency. Your body is like a rubber band. The more you stretch it the more it expands. Spending time exercising increases your energy.

Once in a while I'll say to Ashley, "Word of the week . . . energy!" In other words, "It's going to be a high-energy week. We can't feel down; there's too much to be done. Let's keep moving." How about you? How's your energy?

## CHEER FOR OTHERS

When clown training in small groups was over, it was time to put on a show and exhibit what we had learned. The organizers pumped music into the arena, lined us up backstage, and told us to "do our thing." When the curtains opened to the center ring, we put on a show. There was clapping and excitement. We gave it 110 percent. I learned that the number of people who want you to succeed is greater than the number of people who want you to fail. Sure, there are some haters out there, but for the most part, people are rooting for you. When you bring your genuine self and energy to the arena, they want to cheer you on.

Likewise, it's good for you to cheer for others. In his book *How to Win Friends and Influence People* (a book I am convinced that Hoda Kotb from the TODAY show has read and lives by), Carnegie offers six suggestions on cheering for others: (1) become genuinely interested in other people; (2) smile; (3) remember that a person's name is to him or her the sweetest and most important sound; (4) be a good listener—encourage others to talk about themselves; (5) talk in terms of the other person's interests; (6) make the other person feel important and do so sincerely.[1] Let's look at some examples of what that would look like in real time.

1. *Become genuinely interested in other people.* Every comment I made to people along the fence line began with

"It's so good to see you!" and ended with "Thank you for coming!" Dolly Madison, who was known for her elaborate Washington dinner parties, would greet each guest by saying, "At last you're here!"

2. *Smile.* A smile is inviting. One of the things that the TODAY show loved about the butter story was that I wrote, "I just wanted to make people smile." If you want to draw people to you, light up your face with a smile.

3. *Remember that a person's name is to him or her the sweetest and most important sound.* My efforts to remember names has not always paid off. My childhood pastor told me once, "Donny, you need to remember people's names." Unfortunately, I remember locations better than names. One of the things that helps me to remember people's names is to mention them in prayer every day. That way I'm saying their name and connecting with it emotionally.

4. *Be a good listener—encourage others to talk about themselves.* People have stories worth telling. Ask questions that get them talking. I love to hear other people's stories. Everyone is passionate about something. When we listen, our lives are richer and fuller.

5. *Talk in terms of the other person's interests.* No one did this better than Jesus. When He was with fishermen, He would say, "The kingdom of God is like a man going fishing." When He was with a farmer, he would say, "The kingdom of God is like a farmer sowing seed." The golden rule is to "treat others like you want others to treat you." The platinum rule is to "treat others like they want to be treated."

6. *Make the other person feel important and do it sincerely.*
During the parade I thought of doing something, but, luckily,
I didn't follow through. My thought was to give out my phone
number to people who requested selfies. I know now that
would have been a terrible decision, but I genuinely wanted
people to feel as though their presence was valued. Care for
people. They are worth it!

## THREE BIG IDEAS

1. Little things are big things. This concept, though easily
   stated, is hard to grasp. We tend to believe that in order to
   have a large impact we need to do something dramatic and
   big. But there are no big moments without little moments.

2. It's not about the *big;* it's about what you do with the little
   moments that make the difference.

3. Dale Carnegie offers six suggestions on cheering for others:
   (1) become genuinely interested in other people; (2) smile; (3)
   remember that a person's name is to him or her the sweetest
   and most important sound; (4) be a good listener—encourage
   others to talk about themselves; (5) talk in terms of the other
   person's interests; (6) make the other person feel important
   and do so sincerely.

## THREE BIG QUESTIONS

1. Have you ever been in a situation where you felt you didn't belong? How did you respond?

   _____

   _____

2. How do you plan to increase your energy?

   _____

   _____

3. Write the names of people who are your biggest cheerleaders.

   _____

   _____

# EMBRACE BIG MOMENTS

*"Let's have a parade!" –Macy's*

"Calm down, it's just a parade." I said these words to myself, then I scolded myself for lying. "No, it's not just a parade; it's the *Macy's Thanksgiving Day Parade,* the biggest parade in America! Get excited!" The tension between staying calm and getting excited was unbearable. Should I go crazy and post this on social media? Or should I keep my mouth shut? I told my friends, "Please don't say anything about me being in the parade. A grown man wearing a butter costume running down Sixth Avenue in New York

City isn't the image I want to portray to the world." I wanted to experience the parade, but I was nervous about being seen. I know that seems like a flip-flop, but that was my true feeling. Have you ever been in a situation where you were excited on the inside but trying to play it cool on the outside?

I have a T-shirt that says, "Keep Calm and Lead On." I understand the sentiment, but I find the "Keep Calm" mantra to be wrong. Why should we keep calm when anxiety hits? I guess the idea is we can think better when we're calm. But sometimes, trying to tamp down the high emotional state actually creates more anxiety. Our heart races, our mouth becomes dry, we break out in a sweat. Not only is it impossible to calm down, but when someone tells us to do it, our anxiety ramps up.

Wishing I could stay calm in stressful situations piqued my interest about the subject. I came across a study by a Harvard professor, Alison Brooks, who performed a series of experiments on members of her class in three situations: (1) a singing competition, (2) a public-speaking contest, and (3) a math exam. In each situation the class was instructed to tell themselves one of three things: (1) keep calm, (2) get excited, (3) nothing. The goal was to see how they channeled their nervous energy. Here were the results: In all three areas the students that were excited outperformed those attempting to stay calm. Brooks explained that when you're excited, "it primes an opportunity mindset, so you think of all the good things that can happen. You're more likely to make decisions and take actions that will make [good results] likely to occur."[1]

What if we tried to live that out? What if we learned to lean into excitement rather than try to retreat into calmness? I want to be bolder and more authentic. I want my life to be memorable and exciting. We often have no control over life's actions, but we can manage our reactions. So why not lean in and get excited?

## THE DAY IS BEFORE YOU!

I like the portion of Japanese folklore about the house of a thousand mirrors. The story goes that long ago, in a small, faraway village, there was a place known as the House of a Thousand Mirrors. A small dog learned of this place and decided to visit. When the dog arrived, he bounced happily up the stairs to the front door. He looked at the door with his ears lifted high and his tail wagging as fast as it could. To his great surprise, he found himself staring at one thousand other happy little dogs with their tails wagging just as fast as his. He smiled a great smile and one thousand dogs smiled in return. As he left the house, he thought to himself, *This is a wonderful place, I will come back and visit it often.*

In the same village, there was another little dog that wasn't quite so happy. He too decided to visit the house. He slowly climbed the stairs and with lowered head stared suspiciously at the door. He saw a thousand unfriendly dogs staring back at him. He growled and the pack of dogs growled in return. As he left, he thought to himself, *This is a horrible place, and I will never go back there again.* Of course, it wasn't a house filled with one thousand dogs, whether happy or sad. It was simply a house filled with one thousand mirrors.[2] The lesson is that mirrors only reflect what is set before them.

## YOU HAVE TODAY SET BEFORE YOU

Our lives are made up of bad days, average days, good days, better days than yesterday, and either the best day or the worst day ever. Not every day is phenomenal; not every day is humdrum. But whatever the day brings, rest assured that today is the day we have and how we embrace it is our choice.

## TODAY IS A CHOICE

Today is a gift of 86,400 moments. Some will be positive; some will be negative. You may have messed up yesterday. You may have said the wrong words, took a wrong turn, loved the wrong person, reacted the wrong way. Instead of listening, you may have opened your mouth; instead of trusting you may have judged; instead of standing strong you may have given in. But today is a new day!

One of my favorite television personalities was Mister Rogers. He would walk into his house, take off his sweater, and replace it with another sweater. Then he would take off his dress shoes and put on tennis shoes, all while singing this song:

*I have always wanted to have a neighbor just like you,*
*I've always wanted to live in a neighborhood with you.*
*So let's make the most of this beautiful day.*

I chuckled when I read the following diary entry someone wrote about the perspectives of two pets. The dog's diary read,

8:00 AM—Oh boy, dog food! My favorite thing!
9:30 AM—Rode in the car! My favorite thing!
9:40 AM—Walked in the park! My favorite thing!
10:30 AM—Got rubbed and petted! My favorite thing!
12:00 PM—Crunched on milk bones! My favorite thing!
1:00 PM—Played in the yard! My favorite thing!
3:00 PM—Wagged my tail! My favorite thing!
5:00 PM—Gobbled up dinner! My favorite thing!
7:00 PM—Got to play ball! My favorite thing!
8:00 PM—Watched TV with the people! My favorite thing!
11:00 PM—I get to sleep on the bed! My favorite thing!

Then they compared it to the cat's diary:

Day 2,837 of my captivity. My captors continue to taunt me with bizarre little dangling objects. They dine lavishly on fresh meat, while I'm forced to eat dry cereal. Although I make my contempt for the rations perfectly clear, I nevertheless must eat something in order to keep up my strength. The only thing that keeps me going is my dream of escape. In an attempt to disgust them, I once again vomit on the carpet. Today I decapitated a mouse and dropped its headless body at their feet. I had hoped this would strike fear into their hearts, since it clearly demonstrates what I'm capable of. However, they merely made condescending comments about what a "good little hunter" I am.

There was some sort of assembly of their accomplices tonight. I was placed in solitary confinement for the duration of the event. However, I could hear the noises and smell the food. I overheard that my confinement was due to the power of "allergies." I must learn what this means, and how to use it to my advantage. Today I was almost successful in an attempt to assassinate one of my tormentors by weaving around his feet as he was walking. I must try this again tomorrow—but at the top of the stairs.

I am convinced that the other household captives here are flunkies and snitches. The dog receives special privileges. He is regularly released—and seems to be more than willing to return. The bird has got to be an informant. I observe him communicate with the guards regularly. I am certain that he reports my every move. My captors have arranged protective custody for him in an elevated cell. His safety is assured, but I can wait. It's only a matter of time.[3]

The dog. The cat. One was content; the other was conniving. One was at peace; the other was at war. One was grateful; the other was grumpy.

As I stated at the beginning of this chapter, I was excited and nervous about the parade. I could either go timidly through the motions or lean into the tension and embrace the moment. The moment could be a house of a thousand mirrors. It could be a dog or a cat day. The choice was mine. Just like the choice is yours every day.

## THE BUTTER STORY

Finally, "The BUTTER Story." Once I got over my insecurities about telling it, I realized how much fun it was. I hope you enjoy it as well.

Remember our discussion on the importance of traditions in the Willis family? How we take our kids to the Kids Workshop at Home Depot the first Saturday of every month? Well, we have another tradition, and that is going to the Macy's Thanksgiving Day parade. We started this tradition in 2017, and we've seen the parade from three different angles:

> 2017—A random street corner. This was the year of no bathrooms. Have you ever tried to find a public bathroom in New York City? Impossible.

> 2018—The grandstands at Herald Square. This year was freezing cold, but we did get some pretty awesome red beanies to wear.

> 2019—This was the BUTTER YEAR.

The Butter Year was one of the most memorable moments of my life. It happened on Thanksgiving Day 2019 when I was invited to participate in New York City's Macy's Thanksgiving Day Parade. Here's what happened:

## THE DAY BEFORE

Let's start with the day before when we decided that instead of taking the train into the city the day of, it would be easier to stay at a hotel near the staging site. So we went into the city the night before. The only hotel room we could find had one full-size bed. Luckily for us, the grandparents were in town from Louisiana and they took one of our three kids with them into their room. So in our room it was Ashley, Braydon, Claire, and myself tucked away in a full-size bed. I had to be at the staging area at 5:30 AM, so I didn't sleep a wink.

At 5:00 AM, I struggle out of bed and stumble downstairs to see a long line of people waiting to get into the costume area. When I finally get into my costume, I receive a phone call that goes something like this:

> *Ashley*: Donny, I forgot the tickets in the car!
> *Donny*: OK! I'm already in my costume, but I'll take it off and go see what I can do.
> Love you, bye.

I shed the costume, hurry into the hotel lobby, and tell them the situation. I'm told they use a parking garage under Madison Square Garden, which is close to where we are staying. I run down the street and find the parking garage. I urge the man at the desk to let me go find my car, but he wants to bring it to me. "No!" I say. "I don't have time for that. I just want you to take me to it so I can get my wife and kids' grandstand tickets and get back to the hotel." He insists on doing it his way, so I pull out a one-hundred-dollar bill and say, "PLEASE!" Desperate measures for desperate times. He takes me to the car.

I get the tickets, and my aunt, who is also with us, meets me at door of the hotel, snatches the tickets, and delivers them to Ashley. With the first crisis handled, I rush back downstairs to don my costume. Now, if you're sitting there judging us for forgetting the tickets, in my defense we did just drive through abominable New York traffic on Thanksgiving with a five-, three- and one-year-old. A little grace would be great!

## BUTTER ME UP!

As I enter the costume area, I don't know what character I'm going to be that day, so I jokingly ask the costume lady what am I. She says, *"Butter."* I say, "OK, butter me up!" I put on the costume and head toward makeup. The organizers then funnel us toward a loading ramp, and we follow the leader down a tunnel to a bus that will trundle us to West Side of town, the starting point of the parade. We are told to look for an area called "Clown Corner."

The bus ride is interesting because I'm wearing a stick of butter from my neck down past my knees, which means I can't bend. So I have the brilliant idea to take off the costume so I can sit down. Bad idea; I get stuck. Mallory, my butter friend, is trying to help me, but it's no good. Not only is the stick of butter stuck on me, my clown pants have fallen down and everyone—the butter, eggs, and toast, as well as the leaves and flowers, are getting a sizzling show they weren't expecting. But there's nothing I can do about it. If you'd like to see this wonderful show, go to donnywillis.com and find the blog post labeled "Lessons I learned as the Macy's Butter Man." It is a riot that will not disappoint. Many thanks to everyone who helped me get unstuck as well as to the lady dressed like a leaf who thought the moment worthy of filming.

We finally get to Clown Corner. The clock is approaching 9:00 AM. It's GO TIME! We are listening to the overhead speakers and hearing the crowd chant the countdown: "Five, four, three, two, one, LET'S HAVE A PARADE!" They call for the breakfast clowns to take their places, which just so happens to be at the front of the parade. I look around, trying to decide which side of the street I should walk on. I want to be near people, so I just pick a side and start high-fiving everyone on that side of the street. I have one goal: bring a little joy by making people smile. If I can make one person smile, then for me the parade will be a success. I know what it's like to wake up early to obtain a spot on the street. It's not easy, especially with kids. This day is all about them; they deserve the very best I have to offer. They deserve high energy and high fives. I want them to be glad that they came to the parade.

As the parade progresses, I run over to the right side of the street, mentally sectioning off between the streets and doing everything in my power to get the crowd to chant "BUTTER, BUTTER, BUTTER!" I go to the next section and tell my butter joke: "Did you hear the story of the butter?" "NO!" the crowd responds. "SORRY, I can't tell you. You might SPREAD it!"

## "GET OUT OF HERE, YOU BUTTER!"

We get to the infamous moment at Columbus Circle. Al Roker is doing his live shot, and I hear someone with his entourage scream, "Hey BUTTER! Come over here!" I turn and run over there only to hear Al say, "I hate to butter you up, but you've got to move on." I yell, "Happy Butter Thanksgiving!" He gives me a shove, and says, "Get out of here, you butter!" It was a fun moment but I didn't think anything of it. So we made the turn at Sixth Avenue and I went right back to high-fiving and telling my one corny joke.

If you know how New York City is set up, then you'll know that the avenues run north and south and the streets run east and west. Down the east-west streets there's a viewing spot about fifteen yards down, so I run over there, giving high-fives. This consequently puts me way behind my breakfast group. About halfway down Sixth Avenue, around Fifty-first Street, I notice the widening gap. As I'm sprinting to catch up, I come across Al Roker again. I look straight at the camera and, with no speech-writer and no prompts, say, "We're buttering you up! Butter your ham, butter your turkey!" I'm running on pure adrenaline. Al looks directly at the camera and says, "And that's why everybody loves clowns." I fade off to give some more high-fives and fist bumps. Hopefully, I've created some wonderful memories for families everywhere.

We finally get to the last turn onto Thirty-fourth Street. I look around and spot Ashley and the kids and run over to them. She says, "Donny, what happened?" With a look of shock, I say "What?" She points to the big screen. "They keep talking about you, and we heard your voice." I just reply, "I don't know. Gotta run!"

*Side note:* When I first got into the butter costume, I noticed it was pocketless. What did I do? I slid my phone in the collar of my shirt. Right at the start, it fell down into my pants, which was uncomfortable, especially when it kept buzzing like crazy.

We get back to the staging area only to realize my encounters with Al Roker have broken the internet, twitter, Facebook, and Instagram. I show my phone to the person beside me and ask, "Should I go on Twitter?" To which he responds, "YES!" I download Twitter (donnywillis6) and have over two hundred followers within the next couple hours. From friends to celebrities, everyone seems to be loving the moment. That's what I love about it the most—it is something everyone can have a part in and enjoy.

## MOMENTS REVEAL

Our lives are a combination of both great and painful moments. As a matter of fact, after I appeared on the TODAY show (more on that in the next chapter) I received a text that reminded me of a simple truth. The text said,

> I am stepping aside from being a chef professionally due to my current health issues with lupus. So when you said, "It's not the totality of your life and not your identity," that spoke volumes to me, and I know to the world as well.

Since our lives are full of good moments and bad moments, it's best to hold on to those moments like a hot potato . . . long enough to enjoy it, but not long enough for it to burn. Moments do not define you; moments reveal you. "Butter Man" does not define me; instead, I hope it reveals that I'm striving to be a person who will go out of my way to make someone else's life better. Butter Man was not my identity but rather a platform to spread hope and joy in a very sad and unstable world. We live in a world of fear and labels where people are leery of each other. We fear the unknown, and we label what we fear. We define others by their situation, so each time their name is mentioned, the calamity follows.

> "Have you heard about Jacob? What a cheater! He deceived his aged dad."
>
> "There goes Noah, the patriarch who should've known better than to get drunk."
>
> "By the way, I ran into Geraldine today. She just got fired—again. I wonder why she can't keep a job."
>
> "There's Roy, the man who has cancer."

I'd like to tell you that although you'll be remembered in a similar fashion, those labels don't define you. They reveal you.

When I walked away from the parade, my family and I had dinner at a great Italian restaurant in Manhattan. I kissed my wife and hugged my kids and laughed and enjoyed the night. At the end of the day I was a husband and dad. That meant more to me than the viral moment—that hot potato.

## DEALING WITH CRITICISM

Criticism is part of life. You can't escape it unless you're not doing anything interesting. But social media has taken criticism to a new low. Comments can be immediate, vicious, and unfair. For instance, following the parade, I was criticized on social media. Everyone had an opinion, especially people on Twitter. Some thought my interaction with Roker was wonderful. Some thought I was drunk. Some said the cops should have been called. Not being on Twitter in many years, I thought I had to respond to it all. My goal was to not give the people who were stuffed with turkey and watching the moment in slow motion the opportunity to define the moment. I wanted to define it myself. What was my purpose? "I just wanted people to smile. Nothing more, nothing less." The moment was mine to embrace.

Nadine Stair, at age eighty-five, said, "If I had my life to live over again, I'd dare to make more mistakes next time. I'd relax. I'd limber up. I'd be sillier than I've been this trip. I would take fewer things seriously." We dream of great things, but do we fail to pursue because there might be criticism?

When faced with criticism, never go personal or defensive. If someone attacks you, like a bully on the playground, they're trying to goad you into reacting so they can hit you again. Instead, keep your head high and drive them crazy by making them look small. Truth may work slower than social media, but it always prevails. You can acknowledge criticism without responding negatively. Who knows? You might even learn something from it. Reading some of the comments on Twitter actually helped shape my conversations. I could say, "I know some believe [whatever], but here's what really happened. . . ." It's always good to restate what your critic is thinking. Look at it like feedback; it helps you improve. And like the penguins of Madagascar, "Smile and wave, boys. Just smile and wave."

Some caution you to never read the comments. But I do. I read and respond. The people who are trolling you are expecting you to ignore them. The way I see it, they took time out of their twenty-four hours to comment on something you wrote or shared. Their comment may be negative or mean, but they gave you their time. Say something in return. Post a meme. Try to make them laugh. Don't leave them hanging. Engage . . . connect.

Another way to handle criticism is by humor. Donna Brazile, the first woman and first African American to manage a presidential campaign, starts every speech with, "First of all, I've omitted everything of a partisan nature from this speech, so I'm left with 'Thank you and good-bye,' followed by, 'I'm Al Gore's former campaign manager, so no matter how well things go this afternoon, I can't win.'" Hilarious perspective.

## GO BIG OR GO HOME

When I was younger, we would go to Colorado to snow ski. I remember sitting at the top of the mountain with a few friends and a snowboard attached to my feet, facing a big jump. One of my friends had boarded to the bottom of the jump to record. As I pointed my board toward the hill, another friend yelled, "Go big or go home!" With no weaving and as much speed as possible, I hit the hill and attempted to grab the front of the board. Speeding downward, I overextended and went face first into the snow. The video shows me sliding down the mountain in a cloud of snow. It didn't matter that I didn't hit the jump. I went big! My friends were excited because I went big. I smashed my face into the side of the mountain, but I went big!

I came across an article by Anna Wintour, editor-in-chief of *American Vogue*, a position she has held for over thirty years. I was so intrigued by her leadership prowess that I signed up for one of her online classes. A portion of her lesson was "Designers: What it takes to succeed." Obviously, I'm not a fashion designer, but I do design sermons on a weekly basis, and I'm constantly striving to be better. Wintour offered some principles that I believe illustrate my point of "Go big or go home":

> It is important to go as big and bold as possible, especially at the beginning of your career. Be fearless and extreme, because it will help you home in on what's at the core of your brand. That passion and sensibility are what people will keep coming back to you for and identify as the heart of your brand.[4]

When I was in college, the former LSU football coach Les Miles came to Texas to watch a potential recruit. Miles had flown into a small private airport near our campus. I found out when his departing flight was going to take off, went there, and waited to meet him. I was mentally prepared to ask him if I could hop on the plane with him and go back to Baton Rouge to watch the game. He wouldn't have to worry about any details; I would take care of it all. I just wanted to be on the plane.

There were only six people in the airport waiting room when Coach Miles walked through the door. My mouth turned to cotton, and I froze. All I managed to do was ask for a picture, and he graciously obliged. Then he boarded the plane and took off. There are still moments when I convince myself that if I had just asked, there was a 50/50 chance he would've said yes. But I missed the moment. Right then and there I told myself, "If you get an opportunity to do something that is worth writing about, go big!" That's why I like to take advantage of the moment of opportunity, play it to perfection, and then pursue.

Some will think you've gone overboard; others will not. But guess what? It's not their moment; it's yours. And if that little moment becomes the tipping point for a big difference in your life, it's worth it. Don't downplay your excitement. Embrace it. Keep your perspective while following the path to see where it goes.

## THREE BIG IDEAS

1. When faced with a big moment, you have two options: (1) Tamp down your emotions. However, in striving for calmness, you actually create more anxiety. You are focusing on reining in your emotions rather than focusing on the moment. (2) You can lean into your excitement and embrace the moment.

2. Moments do not define you; they reveal you. Whatever is within you will come out when the bright lights shine your way. Something will eventually happen that you will view as a big moment. The question is, what will it reveal about you?

3. Embrace a big moment like a hot potato. Hold it long enough to enjoy it . . . but not long enough for it to burn you. At the end of the day, it is a moment in your life that you will cherish forever, but it doesn't define you. Be careful not to allow a single moment to define the totality of your life.

## THREE BIG QUESTIONS

1. How was your week?

   _____

   _____


2. What was the biggest moment in your life?

   _____

   _____


3. What do you think of when you hear the words "hot potato"?

   _____

   _____

# BUTTER ON TODAY

*Today ... Tomorrow ... ME*

The day after the Thanksgiving parade, I received texts from friends saying, "The TODAY show will probably invite you as a guest." I brushed it off. *Yeah right, that's never going to happen.* But my friends thought so because the excitement was still trending. On Friday morning, Al Roker called into the TODAY show and recounted the story from his viewpoint. I saw that and decided I should tell my side of the story as well. If you don't define your actions, others will happily do it for you. So I wrote a few paragraphs and posted them online. This was the conclusion of the post:

It was an honor to play a part in the Al Roker/Butter Man encounter, the excellent event produced by Macy's, and the first-class coverage by NBC. I was nothing more than a small part of a massive event. I was simply the guy dressed like a stick of butter with the goal of making people smile who had been standing on the street since 5:00 AM. I wanted them to be happy that they came to the Macy's Thanksgiving Day parade.

As stated in the previous chapter, comments on Twitter attributed all kinds of motives for my actions. But my true motive was truly simple—make people have a *butter* day. That mattered both to me and to Macy's. I was thinking about the out-of-town tourists and all the sacrifices they made to attend the parade. Macy's understands that too, and stresses that fact at Clown U. People purchase high-priced tickets to fly into either LaGuardia, JFK, or Newark. Then they pay transportation fees into Manhattan. Once there, they check into pricey hotel rooms that average around three hundred square feet. They get up before dawn on Thanksgiving morning and stand on the street for hours so they can have a good spot to watch the parade. If kids are with them, they bundle their children in coats, gloves, and scarves and wait for a parade that will not get to them until about 9:00 or 10:00 AM. Oh, and no one can use the bathroom either because someone will confiscate your spot. By the time the parade gets to you, you want—*you need*—excitement, not simply a decorated float moving sedately down the street. You want it to be a personal moment. So I made up in my mind I was going to greet as many people as possible and give them a good time. What could I do to make them smile? What could I do to bring joy? Like a five-star restaurant waiter serving joy and smiles on a platter, I wanted to consider others before myself, because service and servanthood matter.

## SERVANT LEADERSHIP

I believe the person who serves well will always have a job. Martin Luther King Jr. said, "Everybody can be great because anybody can serve. You don't have to have a college degree to serve. You don't have to make your subject and verb agree to serve. You don't have to know the second theory of thermodynamics in physics to serve. You only need a heart full of grace. A soul generated by love."[1]

We aren't here to be served; we are here to serve. To illustrate, think about two men in the Bible who had radically different views on this subject: Pilate and Jesus. The same night of Christ's death, both men took basins of water. One man served himself; the other man served others. "When Pilate saw that he was getting nowhere, but that instead an uproar was starting, he took water and washed his hands in front of the crowd. 'I am innocent of this man's blood,' he said. 'It is your responsibility!'" (Matthew 27:24, NIV). But Jesus, the night before His death, called for a basin and proceeded to wash the dirty, dusty feet of His disciples, even the one who later betrayed Him.

Pilate's attitude is prevalent today. The Roman ruler knew his actions weren't right. "Just then, as Pilate was sitting down on the judgment seat, his wife sent him this message: 'Leave that innocent man alone. I suffered through a terrible nightmare about him last night'" (Matthew 27:19, NLT). But Pilate paid no heed and took the easy way out by passing on to others the responsibility that should have been his.

Many people today wash their hands of everything they can. "Somebody else can do it." "Someone else can take the blame." But if you want to make a difference in your world, serving always works. Serving others is asking the question, "What is the big dream in someone else's head and how can I help to make it a reality?"

## THE TIMELINE

*Saturday, November 20, 2019.* I open my Facebook messenger and read, "Hi this is _____ with the TODAY Show. Can we talk?" I'm thinking, "OK, this *is* happening." We get on the call and set up the interview. By the way, the contact person is amazing at her job and one of the coolest people I know.

*Tuesday, December 3, 2019.* I receive a call from a producer at the show. During our thirty-minute chat, I learn he's from Georgia. I'll leave him nameless, but just in case he reads this, "You're awesome! I'm not sure how long it takes to make a friend, but after that phone call, I consider you one." During the call he asks me to submit to the show a mixture of about fifty pictures and videos. This is crazy. Ashley and I hurriedly pour over every Facebook album and old files on Dropbox, trying to come up with enough.

Later that evening Ashley and I jump on the Metro North and take the train into the city. The TODAY show puts us up in a hotel across the street from the studio. I'm not sure if I'm more excited about being on the show or about having a night in the city without my three kids. Luckily, my in-laws are in town and able to take care of the kids. We stop by Rockefeller Center to figure out a fun way to share with our friends that I am going on TODAY. We go by the gift shop and purchase a TODAY coffee mug. The result turns out to be one of my favorite pictures. (You can go to my Facebook to see it, the one with the caption "Today . . . Tomorrow.")

*Wednesday, December 4, 2019.* We set our alarm for 6:00 AM. I don't fall asleep until about 2:00 and wake up at 5:30. I grab my Bible and read a psalm:

> O God, you are my God; I earnestly search for you. My
> soul thirsts for you; my whole body longs for you in
> this parched and weary land where there is no water. I

have seen you in your sanctuary and gazed upon your power and glory. Your unfailing love is better than life itself; how I praise you! I will praise you as long as I live, lifting up my hands to you in prayer. You satisfy me more than the richest feast. I will praise you with songs of joy. (Psalm 63:1–5, NLT)

At 6:54, a lady whom I'll call J sends me a text, letting us know it's time to roll, so we head downstairs. As I enter the lobby, I stick out my hand to the only lady I see and say, 'Hi, J. I'm Donny," only to see J stick her head around a corner I didn't see and say, "I'm over here!" Oops . . .

We walk across the plaza to the studio and go through security to the "green" room (which isn't green) where they have breakfast ready for us. They really do think of everything. And when I tell you they think of everything, I mean it! Read on . . .

## THEORY OF EVERYTHING

I learn the green room is connected to "hair and wardrobe." Someone walks out from wardrobe, looks me over, and says, "Do you mind if I steam your sweater!" Sure. Every detail is running in sync; everyone is on the same page. That's the way it's got to be in order for things to work because in the natural realm everything is related. This forms the premise for the so-called "Theory of Everything," a unifying theory Einstein spent decades seeking. Each atom, molecule, crystal, cell, organ, animal, bird, fish, individual, group, planet, star, and solar system is somehow connected.

If you do a YouTube search on starlings, you may find one of my favorite examples of unity in the animal kingdom. When thousands of starlings fly together, it is called a murmuration, or sometimes referred to as a "dance" of the starlings. In this dance these birds possess an uncommon unity so majestic scientists stagger at the complexity of it all. When a natural enemy attacks, such as a peregrine falcon, the result is breathtaking. The flock synchronizes its flying in even more complex ways designed to confuse the enemy. One starling makes a meal for a predator, but thousands moving in unity makes for an empty plate. Their strength is found in their unity.

In 1885, the World Series of Mule Team Competition was held in Chicago, Illinois. The winning team of mules pulled something like nine thousand pounds. The second-place team pulled slightly less. Then someone got the bright idea to hitch both teams to a sled to see what the two winning teams could pull together—maybe twice the nine thousand pounds? Wrong! They pulled over thirty thousand pounds! Synergy is found in harmony; the total exceeds the sum of the parts. And the TODAY show is a living example of this principle. They think of everything. And when all the pieces come together, they are more than what they would be separately.

Wardrobe is steaming my sweater when people from Macy's show up with a butter costume, saying I'm going to wear it as a teaser with Al before the interview. I put on the costume and walk out of the dressing room to be greeted by the "sound and audio" guy. He places the sound pack between the clown costume and my waist, and I walk toward the plaza. The producer and a few others brief me about a quick promo. I'm to run toward Al and then will be told what to do as we go along. As I'm running back to the studio after the promo, my microphone pack falls between my legs, so I'm running with my knees together, hoping I don't break the mic!

Back at the studio, wardrobe puts me in a dressing room, and there are my clothes, pressed and hung up, ready to go. I change quickly, and a lady from hair and makeup comes and asks to fix my hair. I tell her, "Sure. Good luck working with what you have!" They re-mic me and I walk toward a door marked with a massive sign "Studio 1A."

At that moment I finally get nervous. My heart rate increases; my mouth goes dry. We're standing behind the cameras as the show goes to a commercial break, and then I see Hoda walk toward us, smiling. She gives me a hug and says, "Thank you for coming! We're so happy you're here." I take the opportunity to slide in my congratulations, because I've heard she recently got engaged. Then the producer, who must be sensing my nervousness, leans over to me and says, "Don't stress out. You'll be fine. Just think of yourself as sitting around a table talking with friends." Right then I know everything will be all right.

## DEALING WITH STRESS

I admit I was stressed, but that's nothing new. One doesn't have to be on the TODAY show to feel stressed. The sheer stress of living in today's word is driving millions of people to the point of illness, depression, and self-destruction. Difficulties, disappointments, accidents, disease, misfortune, cruelty, betrayal—they all happen to people at some point in their lives. On top of that, there's the everyday items such as overworking, raising children, maintaining healthy relationships, or dealing with a pandemic in our world. Carrying so much baggage can sink us. Sometimes all we need is for someone to come alongside us and say, "It's going to be all right. Here, let me help you."

## THE INTERVIEW

Savanna, Hoda, Craig, and Al are experts when it comes to conducting interviews and making their guests feel comfortable. I'm sitting beside Craig. Having recently learned that he did voice work for the Washington Nationals World Series documentary, I congratulate him on that, and talk a little baseball.

Here's how TODAY show writer Scott Stump summarized the interview:

> He's the man, the myth, the margarine. Pastor Donny
> Willis, 32, the man dressed as a stick of butter who got
> into a hilarious "feud" with Al Roker that lit up Twitter
> at the Macy's Thanksgiving Day Parade, appeared
> on TODAY Wednesday to talk about how he helped
> spread cheer on the holiday. "There's been so much
> love and positivity that's come out of this, it's been
> a blessing," Willis said. "Honestly, I just wanted to
> make people smile that day."
>
> His relentless pursuit of Al during the parade
> resulted in moments that had people cracking up to
> start their holiday. "Get out of here, you butter!" Al
> roared in one moment, which even had "Hamilton"
> star Lin-Manuel Miranda tweeting it out. "You but-
> ter believe I did,'" Al tweeted in response. "That guy
> is toast."
>
> Willis, who is a pastor at Westchester Church
> in Valhalla, New York, got involved in the parade
> through a good friend who works for Macy's. The
> father of three didn't know he was going to be dressed
> in that costume until the morning of the parade, but
> he took to the role like butter on toast.
>
> "In the aftermath, I would say that one of the
> biggest lessons is embrace big moments like a hot
> potato,'" he said. "Enjoy the moment . . . but at the end
> of the day, don't hold on to it so much that it becomes
> your identity because it's a singular moment, and it's
> not the totality of your life."

His daughter and two sons are all under 6, so they didn't fully grasp their father melting Twitter on Thanksgiving. "They haven't figured out dad is going to be the most embarrassing thing in their life yet," he said. He also plans on buttering up the crowd again next year.

"Twitter says I need to be there," he joked. As for Al, he wanted it noted for the record that there is no actual feud with the butter man. "I want people to make sure, there was no enmity," Al said on TODAY Wednesday. "Especially now that we know he's a man of the cloth. He's pastor-ized."[2]

Some clichés stick around because they're true. One of my favorites is "Today is a present." So live in the moment and take away what you can.

After the interview, I'm escorted out of the room to find the studio has booked a car to take me wherever I need to go. As I'm exiting the studio into a hallway, I feel a tap on my shoulder. I glance around and wave, thinking, *That looks like Taylor Swift. I didn't realize she was that tall.* Exiting the building, I receive a text from one of the producers letting me know that I was a big hit and I had just received a shout out on air from their next guest—the tall girl that looked like Taylor Swift. Her name is Karli Kloss, who's a big deal in the fashion world. The text said she was lamenting about the fact that she had to follow the Butter Man. But she brings the hosts gifts, and she does well. "Karli, if you ever read this, great job on your interview, and thanks for the shout out."

As we sit in the car, Ashley's phone rings with a request for an interview with Laura Haefeli from *News 12* in Westchester. We've had grandparents staying with us, watching our kids, but it's time for them to fly back home. We drop the kids off at daycare and head for the next interview.

Laura conducts an amazing interview. Here's her summary:

Pastor Donny Willis of the Westchester Church is proof that there really are no small parts.

"I get to the staging area Thursday morning, and I asked the lady doing the costumes and she's like, uh . . . you're butter,'" Willis recalls when he was chosen to play the sandwich spread in the Macy's Thanksgiving Day Parade.

"People woke up at five o'clock in the morning to be there, so I mean if those people are going to make that kind of sacrifice, you have to give it everything you got." Willis adds he was fully committed to the role, so much in fact, that he got the attention of "Today" weather anchor Al Roker during a live broadcast of the parade.

"As we're walking down the parade on Central Park West, we get to Columbus Circle and I'm just running along giving high-fives to people," Willis says when he heard the TV personality's voice call him over: "Hey! I hate to butter you up, but you've got to move on!"

And then there was a second encounter, when he fell behind his parade group and he was hurrying to catch up. "And so I start sprinting, and I guess right before then, Al comes from the other side of the street," Willis said. "Woah! Butter your turkey! Butter your ham!" Willis shouted during the broadcast of the event as he ran to catch up with his group, to which Roker quipped, "And that's why everybody loves clowns."

And now Pastor Willis has gone viral, thanks in part to tweets from the likes of Lin-Manuel Miranda and Al Roker himself. "I got to be in the parade and

it was a lot of fun," Willis says. And if Macy's asks
him back next year, he says he'll be prepared with all
the jokes.[3]

Such a fun day; so many fun moments! But it's time to drop the
hot potato. We stop by daycare and school to pick up our kids,
just like every other parent.

## BEYOND TODAY

The TODAY experience was so wonderful that I wanted to
express my gratitude, so I wrote them a handwritten letter. It
wasn't anything fancy, but it was from the heart. I know they
have multiple guests a day, and from their view I was simply a
five-minute slot. Even so, I was thankful for the opportunity. I
kept in contact with one of the producers, and he and I planned
to have coffee. He invited me to run by the studio, so I did. He
met me at the door, saying, "Come in, you've got to see this." As
I walked in the door, I spotted my photo and letter, framed and
hanging on the wall in a spot where everyone who enters the
studio will see it. He told me they loved it so much they wanted
to find a great place for it. The letter wasn't that amazing, but I
meant every word. It was like going the second mile.

The phrase kept running through my head: "The second
mile makes all the difference." I did some reading on armed
forces medals—Bronze Star, Distinguished Flying Cross, Legion
of Merit, Purple Heart, Silver Star, Navy Cross, the Medal of
Honor to name a few. The criteria for the medals caught my
interest: PERFORMANCE OF NORMAL DUTY WILL NOT JUSTIFY AN
AWARD FOR THIS DECORATION. In other words, you have to carry
your commitment farther than what's required to be considered
for such a medal. If you want your life to be beyond memorable,
go the second mile. There's not much traffic there.

## THREE BIG IDEAS

1. Be genuinely you. Before the TODAY interview, I talked to my brother and asked if he had any advice. He said, "Donny, people recognize and love genuine people. Just be you, and you'll be fine. People will love you." Da Vinci painted only one version of Mona Lisa. Beethoven composed only one Fifth Symphony. And God created only one version of you. So BE YOU!

2. Do your homework. Before I walked into the studio, I researched every person I possibly could and found one positive thing in their life. If the moment arose, I would be ready to make the most of it. I also watched other interviews so I would know what to expect. As one popular quote says, "Those who fail to prepare, prepare to fail."

3. Be extra. A few days after the show, I sent by snail mail a handwritten note thanking everyone who had anything to do with me being there. When someone does something kind for you, go out of your way. Be extra and say thank you. Jesus called this going the second mile.

## THREE BIG QUESTIONS

1. What does "be genuinely you" mean to you?

   _____

   _____

2. What moment are you looking at right now that requires a little extra work?

   _____

   _____

3. How can you go the extra mile?

   _____

   _____

# PART 4
## THE BEST TOMORROW

Photographers call it the golden hour, the time around sunrise or sunset. It's primetime for taking the most beautiful photographs. Why is that? Apparently, the lighting is softer, more diffused, and warmer in hue. To reach the object of the photograph, the light travels through the atmosphere, making the object glow. Shadows are quite pronounced as a result of the sun being so close to the horizon.

It is possible to pursue good things but never pursue the best things. What are the best things in life? Honoring legacies and building legacies. The good book says, "A good man will leave an inheritance [legacy] for his children's children." You will leave a legacy of your life. What type of legacy will it be? That decision is 100 percent yours.

# PART 4

## THE BEST TOMORROW

# BUILDING UPON LAID FOUNDATIONS

*"My brother Roy runs this company.*
*I just piddle around." –Walt Disney*

This book would not have happened without Al Roker. Some people on Twitter thought those encounters were staged, but Al and I had never met until that infamous first moment at Columbus Circle when Al was doing his stand-up bit and I heard someone from his entourage scream, "Hey, BUTTER! Come here!" So I turned and ran over there. The man told some corny butter jokes, then Al said, "I hate to butter you up, but you gotta move on." I yelled, "Happy Butter Thanksgiving!" He gave me a shove and yelled, "Get out of here, you butter!" Al commented, "Argh! I can't believe it's not butter!"

That moment went viral . . . and even became a cool meme. But I'd like to draw something deeper from this experience, and that is to remember that everything has a source. That moment never would have happened if the leadership of Macy's hadn't worked tirelessly to put on a great production and if Al Roker hadn't put in years of service. When you go to the parade as well as the pre-events, like seeing the balloons being blown up, you realize it takes all of Manhattan Island to host and produce that parade.

I believe in giving credit where credit is due: This book never would have been written if it weren't for all the people who played a part in my big moment. *Thank you!*

## LEGACY

The topic of "legacy" comes to mind more often as we get older. It's certainly a topic worth pondering. What will our legacy be? Will we make an impact on our world? Two observations about the subject are (1) we continue the legacy of those who have gone before us, and (2) we build on that legacy for those who come behind us.

If you could write your own obituary, what would it say? Which accomplishment would you highlight? What would be your greatest moment? I think back to the story of my great-grandparents planting the church in Moss Bluff and all the people's lives that are better because of that decision. Only eternity will tell the story.

All of us should desire to leave a legacy, one that paves the way for someone else. In our consumer-driver world, we should have the same desire that President John F. Kennedy so eloquently stated, "Ask not what your country can do for you—ask what you can do for your country." We should transition from being ladder-climbers to ladder-builders. From life consumers to life investors. The remainder of this chapter contains stories of people whose legacies centered on how they honored, lived, sacrificed, and gave their lives for others.

## HONORING OTHERS

It's a common enough theme in life—walking in another man's shoes. We're told if we want to truly understand someone, we must walk a mile in that person's shoes. Sometimes this takes on a new dimension because of the astounding things people have accomplished in borrowed shoes.

For instance, Billy Mills ran the 10,000-meter race in the 1964 Olympics. The US Olympic Committee refused to provide him shoes for the race, saying they had only enough shoes for those they expected to do well. Billy borrowed someone else's shoes and became the only American to ever win the gold medal in this event. He won the race in another man's shoes.

In his major league debut for the Saint Louis Cardinals, Dizzy Dean pitched a three-hitter in a pair of shoes he had borrowed from a teammate. He won in another man's shoes.

Over thirty years ago, the Vietnamese city of Saigon fell to communism. When the North Vietnamese army arrived in the city, one soldier walked into the center of the street, laid down his heavy pack, and gently withdrew an unworn pair of Oxford wingtip shoes, which he had carried around for seven years in fulfillment of a promise made to a dying friend. When his friend had purchased the shoes, he had said, "When I put on these shoes in Saigon, it will mean the war is over. I will dance through the street in these shoes." The shrapnel of an exploding grenade killed him, but not before he extracted a promise from his friend to carry the shoes until the end of the war and then dance through the streets of Saigon in his shoes. The war was over, and it was time to dance. Malnourished and poorly clothed, the man slipped off his filthy sandals and put on the ill-fitting new shoes. Slowly, rhythmically, almost worshipfully, he danced. He danced through the streets of Saigon. He danced in another man's shoes.

Each one of us is walking a road that others have paved before us, and those mentors help us achieve our dreams. The individuals fate places unexpectedly in our path should always be honored. For me and the "butter story," that man was the media icon Al Roker.

Al has been at NBC for over forty years and has covered the Macy's Thanksgiving Day parade for about twenty-five of those years. A New Yorker since birth, Al has been a staple for American families for decades. And, as fate would have it, he placed an opportunity in my life that set off a chain reaction of events that paved the way to the realization of my dreams. No one has ever got to where they are in life without someone else paving the way for them.

## HELPING OTHERS

The other day while bike riding, I passed a massive horse farm with a stately house situated on a hill. The scene was absolutely beautiful. Curious about the owner, I stopped riding, pulled out my phone, and did some googling. The 750-acre farm and about a hundred horses belonged to Barry and Sheryl Schwartz. Barry's story was interesting. He grew up in a one-bedroom apartment in The Bronx. His father owned a local grocery store, and his best friend was a kid named Calvin. When Barry was twenty-one, his father was brutally stabbed to death and thrown in the store's freezer. Barry then took over his father's store, but in 1968 everything changed. I read the rest of Barry's story in an article by Joyce Wadler of the *New York Times*:

The Rev. Martin Luther King Jr. has been assassinated; there is rioting in Harlem. Mr. Schwartz, going up to the family store, finds it ransacked.

[Mr. Schwartz says,] "I call up Calvin and say, 'I'm not coming back here.'" He says, "You can't do that because the store is [supposed] to be our safety net." He comes [over]. [Schwartz continues], "There's very little left, but we fill a couple of shopping bags. I remember he took some sardines; Calvin always loved sardines. I went out on the sidewalk, took the keys, threw them into the store, went downtown, and went in [business] with Calvin. From every bad, no matter how bad, some good comes."

What good was Barry talking about? "I'll give it to you very quickly," Mr. Schwartz says . . . "My father had a supermarket in Harlem. In '68, I gave Calvin $10,000 to make a half-dozen samples and start the company."[1]

I doubt you know who Barry Schwartz is, but I think you'll recognize the name of his childhood friend to whom he loaned $10,000. Does the name Calvin Klein ring a bell? I feel like dropping a famous line from radio legend Paul Harvey, *"And now you know the rest of the story."*

This story illustrates how one person can make all the difference. No one is self-made. Anyone worth following will quickly point out someone else who influenced them, trained them, managed them, or helped them get from point A to point B.

## CONNECTING TO OTHERS

Our lives are changed according to the connections we make. A few weeks ago, my wife and I took the two-and-a-half-hour ride from our house to Boston, a town rich with American history. As we were walking around Boston Commons, Ashley decided she wanted to shop. I, on the other hand, wanted to follow the Freedom Trail. So I stepped into a gift shop, purchased a book on the trail, and began a self-guided tour. The trail is a brick walkway running down the middle of the sidewalk that weaves its way throughout downtown Boston, passing various historic sites like the Boston Massacre, site of the 1770 riot on King Street, and the grave of Paul Revere. I spent a lot of time at the Old North Church, which was used to alert the patriots of British Army movements. They would hang lanterns in the belltower—one if by land, two if by sea. In the church courtyard was a plaque honoring the midnight ride of Paul Revere: "Paul Revere—Patriot, Master Craftsman, Good Citizen." At the bottom of the plaque I saw another name: William Dawes, and wondered how these two men were connected. Why does history tell Revere's story, but Dawes's name is only a blimp at the bottom of Revere's plaque?

The answer is that Revere was not the only one who rode on that April night; Dawes did too. Revere rode north and Dawes rode south. Both men carried the message, "The British are coming!" That's where the connection ends because Revere's message spread like a fire in a dry forest, and Dawes's message spread like fire in the middle of a rainstorm. Revere's message reached Lincoln, Massachusetts, by 1:00 AM., Sudbury by 3:00 AM, Andover (forty miles northwest of Boston) by 5:00 AM, and as far as Ashby (near Worcester) by 9:00 AM. When the British finally began their march toward Lexington, they were met—to their utter astonishment—with organized and fierce resistance.

William Dawes, on the other hand, carrying an identical message, worked his way south through as many towns and over as many miles as Paul Revere. But his ride didn't have the same impact. In fact, the people in Waltham didn't find out the British were coming until it was too late.

Why was one ride successful and one not? It goes back to the words inscribed on Revere's plaque in the yard of the Old North Church: "Good Citizen." Revere was so well-known and well-connected that when he spoke, people listened. Have you ever seen the illustration of the Boston Massacre? Do you know who drew it? I assure you the people of Boston knew; it was Paul Revere. He framed in both words and art the picture that launched the American Revolution.

Paul Revere was well-known before his legendary ride. When Boston imported its first streetlights, Paul Revere served on the committee. When the Boston market required regulations, Revere was the clerk. He founded the Massachusetts Mutual Fire Insurance Company after a major fire ravaged the town. He served in over one hundred different capacities in his life. "It is not surprising, then, that when the British army began its secret campaign in 1774 to root out and destroy the stores of arms and ammunition held by the fledgling revolutionary movement, Revere became a kind of unofficial clearing house for the anti-British forces. He knew everybody."[2]

That's why Paul Revere's midnight ride started a word-of-mouth epidemic and William Dawes's message went in one ear and out the other. Paul Revere was connected with others. He was a fisherman and a hunter, a cardplayer and a theater-lover, a successful businessman and a master craftsman. He was a doer, a man who loved being in the middle of the action. He was trusted. He was loved. He was a son of liberty. When he died, his funeral was attended, in the words of one contemporary newspaper account, by "troops of people." And when the moment arose to change the course of history, he was able to do so because he spent his life connecting with those around him.

You may be familiar with the "six degrees of separation theory," which says two persons chosen at random from distant parts of the world can be connected through a chain of acquaintances of no more than five or six people. That may be true. But not all connections are equal. Some have "a special gift for bringing the world together." They are people who love to connect. Connectors do not necessarily start revolutions, but they facilitate the process. Connect with others and change the world.

## LIVING FOR OTHERS

The headline of the *Hudson Dispatch* read, "Harrowing Tale of Scenes on Titanic by Miss Dowdell." The subhead proclaimed, "Many men sacrificed their lives in forming human ladder to help women and children to lifeboats."[3] Elizabeth Dowdell was a passenger on the Titanic. She was governess to the six-year-old daughter of Mrs. Estelle Emanuel, a famous opera singer. When the Titanic began to sink, Elizabeth snatched up Virginia and worked her way through the panicked crowds. The screaming was so loud that a single voice could hardly be heard. When the final lifeboat started to be lowered, Elizabeth fought to get her young charge aboard. Early on, panic had resulted in partially loaded lifeboats being lowered into the water. Now, there was no space for everyone who wished to escape the ship. One man saw Elizabeth attempting to save little Virginia. He took hold of another man's hands and together they formed a ladder spanning the gap to the lifeboat. Stepping across this human ladder, Elizabeth carried Virginia to her salvation.

She wrote, "Much should be said for the noble and heroic acts on the part of the men, and should ever remain in the reminiscences of the history of the world. Many a social leader or man of wealth grasped hold of the limbs of a laborer and sacrificed his life just to form the human ladder where woman and child escaped from perishing." Then, speaking of a particular man who had helped them as he was dying, "See here little girl [Virginia]; step on my face and be saved." Elizabeth wrote, "I will never forget him . . . for he did die nobly."[4]

## SACRIFICING FOR OTHERS

In September 1992, Jack Kelley, foreign affairs editor for *USA Today*, witnessed firsthand the famine in Somalia. One starving boy touched Kelley: "Our photographer had a grapefruit, which he gave to the boy. The boy was so weak he didn't have the strength to hold the grapefruit, so we cut it in half and gave it to him. He picked it up, looked at us as if to say thanks, and began to walk back towards his village.

"We walked behind him in a way that he couldn't see us. When he entered the village, there on the ground was a little boy who I thought was dead. His eyes were completely glazed over. It turned out that this was his younger brother. The older brother kneeled down next to his younger brother, bit off a piece of the grapefruit, and chewed it. Then he opened up his younger brother's mouth, put the grapefruit in, and worked his brother's jaw up and down. Jack learned that the older brother had been doing that for the younger brother for two weeks. A couple days later the older brother died of malnutrition, and the younger brother lived."

## EMPATHY FOR OTHERS

A few days ago, I was reading one of my journal entries from 2010 when I was a student pastor. The entry read,

> Over the last week and a half I have experienced more broken moments than some years combined. In 7 days I visited 6 individuals in 5 different hospitals. I experienced things such as walking with a student into the ICU so that he could be in the room when his

grandfather took his last breath, to another moment
of consoling a student who attempted to take his own
life only to find his mother and father not at the hospital with him, only his neighbor.

Fast forward to August 18, 2016, when I was an assistant pastor
and Louisiana was experiencing the aftermath of the "great flood
of 2016." I drove to a suburb of Baton Rouge, Louisiana, to help a
friend who was affected by the flood. We pulled everything out of
his home and placed it on the side of the road. Like everyone else,
the walls of his house had watermarks as high as six feet. We took
hammers and slammed them into the wall to create a hole, then
we would rip the sheetrock off the walls. As I was leaving, he said,
"There has to be a silver-lining here somewhere."

Stories like this are very personal to me. I can still remember the names, recall the sights, and feel the raw emotion. Two
particular days are burned into my memory to the point I can
relate every detail. One of those days is so personal I can't share
it, but I'd like to share some of the details of the other day and
lessons I learned from the experience. The day was January 10,
2018, one of the hardest days of my life.

I had been pastor for only 284 days. We had moved to New
York on April 1, 2017, and the first two months we lived in a
friend's church apartment in Long Island. The next two months
we lived in a cheap hotel room in Stanford, Connecticut. Finally,
in August, we moved into our house and began settling in. We
began building relationships, focusing on growing a church,
and finding, to our joy, that Ashley was pregnant. In the midst of
all this, I met a man and convinced him that we needed to do a
Bible study together, so we started in October. In our discussions
I discovered he shared as much about the Bible as I did. He also
was a lover of rock music.

One of the things the man shared is that the Bible is a dictionary containing the names of heavy metal rock bands. Exodus isn't a group of people wandering in a desert; it's a rock band. Nine Inch Nails has nothing to do with Jesus; it's a rock band. Lamb of God, Testament, and Avenged 7-fold have nothing to do with the judgment of God; they're rock bands. Nazareth wasn't Jesus' hometown and King James isn't a version of the Bible; you guessed it . . . they're rock bands. I loved spending time with the guy. Then on January 10, 2017, I went to his house, like always, and knocked on the door. His dad answered: "Hey Don, does he know you're here?"

"He should. We chatted last night."

"Well, he's still asleep. Feel free to wake him up."

We go upstairs to his room, and as we open the door, we see his body lying there completely still and lifeless. He had died in his sleep. His dad jumped on him and started CPR. I ripped my phone out of my pocket and called 911. I spent the next few hours on the porch as police, paramedics, and other officials came in and out of the house. I can still feel the emotion of those moments.

The next few weeks were filled with the memorial service, counseling sessions, and many unanswered questions. For me, many years later, there are still some unanswered questions. But I did learn some things I would like to share with you. Through every hardship, there's one quality that continues to rise to the top—empathy.

As I researched the subject, I came across a TED talk by researcher and writer Brené Brown in which she discusses the difference between sympathy and empathy. She says one of the things we do when facing a difficult conversation is to try to make things better. We attempt to create a silver lining around the situation by using the words "at least."

Someone says, "My son is failing in school." Reply: "But at least your daughter is an A student."

"My marriage is falling apart." Reply: "At least you have a marriage."

"My friend passed away." Reply: "At least you have more friends."

"I had a miscarriage." Reply: "At least you can get pregnant again."

"I lost my dad." Reply: "At least you still have your mom."

"I got laid off my job." Reply: "At least you know you can get another job."[5]

Brown said, "If I share something with you that is very difficult I would rather you say 'I don't even know what to say right now, I'm just glad you told me.' Because the truth is, rarely, can a response make something better. What makes something better is connection."[6] The world we live in is nothing more than a shadow of the greater world that is within us. That's where a person really lives—within.

What is the flooding of a river compared to the tears that flood our face? What is the destruction of a tornado compared to the breaking of our heart? What is the blasting of a mountain compared to the crushing of our spirit? What is the pounding of a hurricane compared to the storms that brutalize our emotions?

You can't fix every problem, but you can always have empathy.

## FOLLOW THE STONES

One of most impactful sermons I ever heard was called "Follow the Stones." It references a story that I believe is the embodiment of legacy. Douglas McCarren was a CIA employee in Kiwa, China, in 1949 as the Communist Party was taking over the country. McCarren was rushing to destroy important documents when he found out normal modes of transportation had been cut off. So he and four companions mounted horses and trekked 1,200 miles across the Taklamakan Desert. The name in Chinese means "go in and you won't come out." They nearly died of thirst traveling three days without water until they found a small stream.

After surviving the desert, they came to the base of the Himalayas, which they had to cross to reach the safety of Tibet. The path through the mountains had been well established a hundred years prior, but it was the dead of winter and fierce mountain winds had piled snowdrifts over the path, obscuring their way. Frostbite set in, blinding McCarren in one eye. His horse died; his shoes were torn. But when, at every remote village and every outpost he asked, "Am I still on the path? Is this still the right way?" he always got the same answer: "Follow the stones." At times McCarren had to backtrack to make sure he was on the right path. He had to "follow the stones" or he would lose his life.

The ground in the Himalayas is always frozen, always hard. So when travelers died, there was no way to bury them; they would pile stones over the travelers where they fell. The stone graves became the *trail markers*, the legacy left behind by travelers in the past.

One night I began to consider this story and thought about the phrase "we live in unprecedented times." I'm sure you've heard that said by politicians, the media, or your neighbor. Let me put your mind at ease; we don't live in unprecedented times. We've always had stones to follow, past travelers on the journey through life. They may not have made it as far as we, but without them we wouldn't be where we are today. I doubt that the challenges we confront are any worse, or even that different, than the challenges previous generations have faced. The wise man said, "There is nothing new under the sun." So keep going and follow the stones. They are your legacy.

## WHEN THE GAME IS OVER

An out-of-work salesman named Charles Darrow had a bright idea. It was during the Great Depression, a dark time in American history. There was great financial difficulty, great struggle. People had no money—but they did have time on their hands. Darrow was approached by two brothers, George and Charles, who wanted to capitalize on the moment. They found a way to help people escape for two to three hours by giving them the feeling that they were rich in the midst of depression. In 1935, these brothers approached Darwin and asked him to sell them his idea. George and Charles Parker patented the game of Monopoly, which has sold millions of copies.[7] Monopoly currently is the fourth highest-selling board game of all time. It's fun to play—if you know how to play.

In order to win at Monopoly, you have to take risks. You have to play to win. You spend every dollar, you buy every piece of property, you mortgage everything to the hilt in order to buy everything else. Accumulating is the name of the game; money is how you keep score; the race goes to the swift. It's a game you play with passion, skill, and reckless abandon. The goal is to basically own everything, to have total control.

Everyone else sitting around the table sees your stack of mortgages and cash, and they realize you are untouchable. The more you have the more insulated you become from the attacks of others. When you own Boardwalk and Park Place, life is good. Others who land on those blue spots are handing over everything they have left. You are the big cheese.

Then something unique and interesting happens at the end of the game. Whether you owned the Boardwalk or the first purple square; whether you were the winner or the loser, everything goes back in the box. All of the cash goes back in the box. All of the characters go back in the box. All of the mortgages go back in the box. Because when the game is over, everything goes back in the box.

Life is like a game of Monopoly. We strategize and "wheel and deal" to improve our position. We speed around the board with frantic schedules and shallow relationships. We accumulate temporary rewards that lull us into thinking the game will go on forever. But when the game is over, all the pieces go back in the box. The only things that remain are the memories and the legacy we leave. If the game isn't about you, it will live beyond you.

## THREE BIG IDEAS

1. No one has ever progressed to their present position in life without someone else paving the way for them.

2. You aren't responsible for knowing everything, but you are responsible for sharing everything you know. There are people around you desiring to "do" life with you, glean from you, and emulate you. So pour into them and reproduce yourself.

3. Walt Disney, John F. Kennedy, and Martin Luther King Jr. were successful because (1) they shared their dream with others, and (2) the dream wasn't about them. If your life isn't all about you, it will live beyond you.

## THREE BIG QUESTIONS

1. Who is the one person in your life that paved a way for you?

   _____

   _____

2. What person are you paving the way for?

   _____

   _____

3. What transition do you need to make to change from a road traveler to a road builder?

   _____

   _____

# HOT POTATO

*Hot Potato – A Moment in your life not the totality of your life. –Donny Willis*

It doesn't matter how or where you start; it matters how or where you finish. The greatest disservice to yourself is to not finish strong. Having the desire to see your business grow, your ability increased, your dreams power-packed with passion is only the beginning. Desire isn't enough. You must finish faithfully and finish well.

I coached track and field for one season at a high school in Louisiana. We were at a JV meet the first of the year, and the track meet was coming down to the final events, one of which was the mile—about 1600 meters. One of our runners was a kid who was kind of lazy; he usually came to practice, but he didn't really practice. He never gave it his all. My expectations for him weren't that high.

The event was coming to a close, and it was time for him to run the mile. The runners took their marks. The gun was raised and fired—BOOM! The runners blasted off the lines. I was standing with the long-distance coach and the other coaches when someone asked, "Hey, where's our guy?" The runners had already gone a half of a lap when our guy showed up and asked, "Coach, did my race start yet?" The long-distance coach grabbed him and threw him on the track. "Get to running!" Three-quarters of a lap from the start, our guy was on the track and everyone on the infield was laughing at the theatrics:

One lap down—our guy is last.

Two laps down—our guy catches the back of the pack.

Three laps down—our guy is in the middle of the pack.

Three and one-half laps down—our guy is in fourth place.

Three and three-quarter laps down—our guy is in second place.

With about fifty meters to go, our guy passes the first-place runner.

When the race is over, he jogs off the track, asking, "Coach, did I make good time?"

The long-distance coach just stood there in disbelief. He pointed to the bus and said, "You can go get on the bus."

## FINISH WELL

Desire should be at the core of our lives. It's the fuel that propels us out of lethargy. Desire should churn within us like volcanic action: it pushes and pulls; it draws and shoves. But desire isn't enough. When the wise man wrote, "The desire accomplished is sweet to the soul" (Proverbs 13:19), he was saying, "The thorough fulfillment of your desire brings a feeling of satisfaction that cannot be expressed in words." Webster's Dictionary defines "thorough" as "carried through to completion, careful about detail, complete in all respects."

Kerri Strug was a member of the Magnificent Seven, the victorious all-around women's gymnastics team that represented the United States at the Atlanta Olympics in 1996. She is best remembered for performing the vault despite having injured her ankle and for subsequently being carried to the podium by her coach, Béla Károlyi. Sometimes you have to "play" hurt. Desire must be greater than the pain.

The 1968 Summer Olympic Games were held in Mexico City. On October 20, thousands of spectators in the stadium witnessed Ethiopia's Degaga "Mamo" Wolde win the marathon. The sun went down and people began gathering their things and exiting the stadium. Then around 7:00 PM, over an hour after Wolde's win, something unusual happened. Those sitting near the entrance gates heard sirens and police whistles. All eyes turned to the gate and watched as John Akhwari entered the stadium, grimacing with every step. They looked closer and saw that John's leg was bloody and bandaged. It was learned later that during the race he had cramped up due to the high altitude in the city. He had never trained at such an altitude in Tanzania, his home country. The cramping caused a terrible fall that dislocated and wounded his knee. When he finally crossed the finish line, a cheer arose from the few thousand remaining spectators. A television interviewer asked

John why he kept going. He replied, "My country did not send me 7,000 miles to start the race. They sent me 7,000 miles to finish it."[1]

How we finish matters, especially in life. The Book of Job (NKJV) paints many pictures of the brevity of life:

- "My days are swifter than a weaver's shuttle" (7:6).
- "As the cloud disappears and vanishes away, so he who goes down to the grave does not come up" (7:9).
- "Our days on earth are a shadow" (8:9).
- "Now my days are swifter than a runner" (9:25), referring to the royal couriers that hastened in their missions.
- "[My days] pass by like swift ships, like an eagle swooping on its prey" (9:26).
- "Man who is born of a woman is of few days, and full of trouble. He comes forth like a flower and fades away; he flees like a shadow, and does not continue" (14:1–2).

We are transients; our life is like a journey. Oliver Wendell Holmes said, "Many people die with their music still in them. Too often it is because they are always getting ready to live. Before they know it, time runs out." Since life is so brief, we can't afford to spend it frivolously, and we certainly don't want to waste it. We must invest our life and finish well.

This book suggests there is a way to get from where you are to where you want to be, but sometimes you don't end up where you want to be. You can try retracing your steps and making better choices next time, but bad decisions and setbacks may move your destination out of reach. Reality strikes and you find yourself back to square one. The journey comes at a cost. I'm not just speaking financially, though it does do that. Instead, I'm referring to time, energy, emotion, and relationships. Pursuing your dream requires things of you. As in real estate, there are known costs—and then there are hidden costs lurking beneath the surface that must be taken care of to finish well.

Consider the tragedy involving the Space Shuttle *Columbia*. The *Columbia* represented the scientific accomplishment of some of the best minds in America. The crew was surrounded by approximately one billion dollars of NASA equipment with many times that amount supporting them on the ground. It had been a successful mission. Things were stowed away. Family and friends were waiting in Florida for their return. Then, only fifteen minutes away from their destination, the unthinkable happened. The shuttle disintegrated as it reentered earth's atmosphere and seven lives were lost. So close, but so far away. One can start right and continue that way for a length of time. But it's the end of the journey that we must secure.

*The Road Less Traveled* starts out with the three-word phrase, "Life is difficult." I know a lot of people who share that sentiment, because life can be hard, and there's a major temptation to just get by. But those who are satisfied to do only what is required will never make a difference. In our age of apathy, where many are just doing enough to get by, the challenge is to not get caught up in the same mindset that affects the nation, the family, the workplace, and the classroom. Anyone can be ordinary. Anyone can just go the proverbial one mile. But the one-milers never see the rewards that come with sacrifice. Be a two-miler and experience the extraordinary. Go the second mile and finish well.

## RELOAD!

I was picking up a friend from LaGuardia Airport when I noticed a sign outside of the loading dock that said, "Parking for Loading and Unloading Only." It meant, "You can park here long enough to make preparation to move on, but you can't stay here!" It seems that every time you just get settled on a new plateau and begin enjoying your success, you look around and see a sign that says, "Parking for Loading and Unloading Only."

After the Revolutionary War, some Americas doubted that the newly freed colonies could govern themselves. In May 1782, George Washington received a letter from Colonel Lewis Nicola, one of his officers, proposing that the general use the army to make himself king of the United States. Washington's response on May 22 was sharp:

> With a mixture of great surprise and astonishment I have read with attention the Sentiments you have submitted to my perusal. Be assured, Sir, no occurrence in the course of the War, has given me more painful sensations than your information of there being such ideas existing in the Army as you have expressed, and I must view with abhorrence, and reprehend with severity. For the present, the communication of them will rest in my own bosom, unless some further agitation of the matter, shall make a disclosure necessary.
>
> I am much at a loss to conceive what part of my conduct could have given encouragement to an address which to me seems big with the greatest mischiefs that can befall my Country. If I am not deceived in the knowledge of myself, you could not have found a person to whom your schemes are more disagreeable. At the same time in justice to my own feeling I must add, that no man possesses a more sincere wish to see ample Justice done to the Army than I do, and as far as my powers and influence, in a constitution[al] way extend, they shall be employed to the utmost of my abilities to effect it, should there be any occasion. Let me [assure] you then, if you have any regard for your Country, concern for your self or posterity—or respect for me, to banish these thoughts from your Mind, and never communicate,

as from yourself, or anyone else, a sentiment of the like nature. With esteem I am Sir Yr Most Obedt Servt

Go. Washington[2]

King George said that if Washington voluntarily gave up power, then he truly would be the greatest man on earth. Oliver Cromwell wouldn't do it. Napoleon wouldn't do it. But Washington did. He might have had a kingdom for the asking, but he was not interested. He held on to the moment, then let it go and moved on. It was time to reload. Life is for loading and unloading only. No Parking. Don't hold on to it any longer than you would a hot potato.

## LET YOUR SUCCESS BEGIN!

Walt Disney, John F. Kennedy, Martin Luther King Jr., and a host of others who joined in the chorus of this book were successful because their dream wasn't all about them. They shared their dream with others, and their dream lived on even after they were gone. If your life is all about you, it will die with you. But if it isn't all about you, it will live on after you're gone. So I ask, "Who are you investing in? Who are you bringing alongside you? Who will inherit your legacy?"

Consider this thought: you are not responsible for knowing everything, but you are responsible for sharing everything you know. There are people around you every day that desire to do life with you, glean from you, and emulate you. Give them a chance and you'll discover how awesome they are.

A few months ago, my family and I watched as NASA and SpaceX sent astronauts to space from American soil for the first time since the end of the shuttle program eleven years prior. Following the countdown, a voice announced, "Godspeed, Bob and Doug." "Godspeed" is an expression of good favor. So, to you I say,

"Your endless frontier isn't space; it's your dreams. May they capture the essence of your life—and I wish you Godspeed on your journey."

Four hundred years ago, *Godspeed* was one of the three ships owned by the English Virginia Company that brought settlers to Jamestown, the first permanent English settlement in North America. The captain wrote in his diary, "She is Thy Ruler of the seas, with her mightyfulle velocitie, moure veloce than the wynd, and mightier than the rocke, she is, my Deare Godspeed."[3] So, my dear friend, may your dreams rule the seas of life with mighty force, and may they churn within you mightier than a rocket. Embrace your destiny. Live life to the fullest. Maintain your integrity. Enjoy the journey, and Godspeed. Good, Butter, Best.

## THREE BIG IDEAS

1. Life is made up of people and places, activities and goals, days and years. At some point each of us must make many crucial decisions. To live a life of value and significance, we must find our life purpose. Life is more than the temporal things to which we assign so much importance. Life is all too brief, so we can't afford to "spend our lives" or "waste our lives." We must invest our lives!

2. This book suggests there is a way to get from where you are to where you want to be, but you don't always end up where you want to be. Sometimes you have to retrace your steps and make better choices next time. The day may come when time, bad decisions, and experiences put your intended destination out of reach and you find yourself back at square one. The journey costs in terms of time, energy, emotion, and relationships.

3. There's always another mountain to climb, pages to be turned, chapters to be written, and lives to be touched. Live life to the fullest. Let your life be full of passion. Carpe Diem—seize the day! Maintain your integrity. And don't forget to enjoy the journey.

## THREE BIG QUESTIONS

1. Who will you invest in?

   _____

   _____


2. What will your legacy be?

   _____

   _____


3. What's next?

   _____

   _____

## THREE BIG QUESTIONS

# THANK YOU

I realize it probably took you only a few hours to read this book but writing it has been like pulling hens' teeth. As I write this paragraph, it's summer. My wife is now principal of her school, and I'm working at home while she prepares for the new school year. I made pancakes this morning and the kitchen is a mess. "Baby Shark" is playing in the background. The distractions in our home are the story of our lives; in fact, with three kids it's a miracle I was able to write this manuscript. But I don't want to end without saying thank you to a few people.

## ASHLEY WILLIS

Thank you for being the constant in my life. You chose to follow me on the 1,300-mile journey to New York and believed in my crazy dream. You are my secret weapon; I believe you could lead the world. You are one of a kind and I love you so much.

## BRAYDON, CLAIRE, ELLIOT

You three are daddy's buddies forever and always. My prayer is that you always love Jesus. Braydon, your intentional focus and attention to detail is a gift. Claire, you are sweet and strong. You can conquer the world if you wish. Elliot, your imagination is enlightening, so stay creative! It will serve you well. Love you all so very much. Dad

## WESTCHESTER CHURCH FAMILY

To my Westchester Church family: You took a risk on a twenty-nine-year-old when you chose me to be your pastor. You've allowed me to make mistakes while learning to lead the church. There is so much joy and love in my heart for you that I could go on and on. But from the bottom of my heart, thank you for accepting us and loving us. You are not just a church; you are our family. I pray for you every day. I love you.

## MOM AND DAD

Thank you for being the biggest cheerleaders in my life. Mom, you post and repost everything I do, and I love it! It's nice to know you are in my corner. Thank you, Dad. Your quiet confidence has led my life. I think about you going to the same office for over thirty years in order to provide for our family and give us a stable life. You are the greatest life example I could ever ask for. Thank you.

## MACY'S FAMILY

To the Macy's family, thank you for allowing me to be a part of your brand. You make the season come alive and inspire us all. Orlando, you do your job so very well. And to whoever runs the social media, thanks for all the posts. You are amazing!

## NAPOLEON AND SUSAN

If it hadn't been for you guys, this work wouldn't have happened. For signing off and sponsoring me to be in the parade to simply being our friend, Ashley and I are thankful for you. Blessings.

## TODAY SHOW FAMILY

Heartfelt thanks for the love and kindness shown to me on your show. I was blown away by the first-class culture you've created and have a greater appreciation for the reason why America loves you.

Special thanks to Al for letting me share the spotlight at the parade and for keeping the trend going long enough to give me a platform from which to write this book. Your consistency and kindness are traits that should be pursued and valued in our world. I will forever be grateful that destiny brought us together for a short time. In a changing world it's wonderful to see someone who displaces faithful consistency. You are the one who paved the way. Congrats on your twenty-fifth parade.

Also, thanks to Katie, Kevin, and Julie. You guys know how to calm nerves and make people feel loved. Maddy, your kindness and professionalism are second to none. Thank you for being you. To the sound guy who kept me from breaking the equipment, well done!

Al, Hoda, Craig, and Savanna, after sitting on the set with you I realized just how amazing you are. Thanks for bringing joy to the world.

## KEVIN @ TODAY

I value your friendship, from the first phone call to the most recent. You care about my opinion and you possess the gift to make people feel like the king of the world. Keep doing what you do. You are phenomenal!

## KATIE @ TODAY

Thanks for the ask! You are amazing at what you do, and NBC is blessed to have you work for them.

## MALLORY

To my butter in crime. I had a blast being butter with you. Thank you for helping me get out of my comfort zone and embracing the day. You're a great friend and a better butter than I.

## CYNTHIA A. LOVELY

Your name depicts your spirit. Thank you for first edits and encouraging me along the way. When we first spoke about the project, you instantly believed in me. Thank you for your kindness and hard work. All the best.

## MRS. PAT BOLLMANN

Thank you to the lady who read every word and made them better. When I read your final edits there was a sense of relief that washed over my mind and emotions. From the bottom of my heart—Thank You!

## TO YOU!

To you who purchased this book, thank you so much for giving me your time. I hope this book made your day *butter!* Every story was chosen with purpose. I didn't want it to be just a thrown-together book; the last thing I want to do is waste your time, the most valuable gift anyone can give. My purpose was to honor you with my writing, and I hope I achieved that. It was all for you—Good. Butter. Best.

# NOTES

## CHAPTER 1–BEYOND YOUR WILDEST DREAM

1. Martin Luther King Jr., "I Have a Dream," speech. American rhetoric. Accessed September 15, 2020, https://www.americanrhetoric.com/speeches/mlkihaveadream.htm.

2. Bill Capodagli and Lynn Jackson, *The Disney Way: Harnessing the Management Secrets of Disney in Your Company* (New York, NY: McGraw-Hill Education, 2016).

3. "Magic Kingdom," Disney Wiki. Accessed September 15, 2020, https://disney.fandom.com/wiki/Magic_Kingdom.

4. Piers Bizony, "'We Choose to Go to the Moon': Read JFK's Moon Speech in Full." *BBC Science Focus*, April 9, 2020, https://www.science-focus.com/space/we-choose-to-go-to-the-moon-read-jfks-moon-speech-in-full/.

5. Brian Dunbar, "July 20, 1969: One Giant Leap for Mankind," NASA, February 19, 2015, https://www.nasa.gov/mission_pages/apollo/apollo11.html.

6. Drew D. Hansen, *The Dream: Martin Luther King, Jr., and the Speech That Inspired a Nation* (New York, NY: Ecco, 2005).

## CHAPTER 2–THE ROOTS OF A DREAM

1. Max Lucado, *You! God's Brand New Idea: Made to Be Amazing* (Nashville, TN: J Countryman Books, 2007).

2. Amy Relich Cuddy, *Presence: Bringing Your Boldest Self to Your Biggest Challenges* (New York, NY: Little, Brown and Company, 2015).

## CHAPTER 3–GROWTH CYCLE OF A DREAM

1.  Josie Bisset, "Dreams come in a size too big so that we may grow into them," passiton.com. Accessed September 15, 2020, https://www.passiton.com/inspirational-quotes/5298-dreams-come-in-a-size-too-big-so-that-we-may.

2.  Andy Stanley, *Visioneering* (Sisters, OR: Multnomah Publishers, 2005).

3.  Andy Cook, "Finding a Purpose in Your Pain," Sermon January 1, 2014, https://www.lifeway.com/en/articles/sermon-purpose-pain-2-corinthians-12.

4.  Bill Capodagli and Lynn Jackson, *The Disney Way: Harnessing the Management Secrets of Disney in Your Company* (New York, NY: McGraw-Hill Education, 2016).

## CHAPTER 4–CHARACTERISTICS OF A DREAMER

1.  Antonin Scalia, eds. Christopher J. Scalia and Edward Whelan, Foreword by R. B. Ginsburg, *Scalia Speaks: Reflections on Law, Faith, and Life Well Lived* (New York, NY: Crown Forum, 2017).

2.  Coach Cleveland Stroud, cited by T. F. Tenney in *Water from an Old Well* (Hazelwood, MO: Word Aflame Press, 2008).

3.  Thomas Carlyle, Brainy Quote.

4.  Bob Hawke, quoted by Steven Covey in *First Things First* (New York, NY: Simon & Schuster, 1995).

5.  Emma Johnson, *How to Eliminate Distractions*, 2016, retrieved July 21, 2020, from https://www.success.com/how-to-eliminate-distractions/

6.  Lori Greiner, quoted by John C. Maxwell in *Leadershift: the 11 Essential Changes Every Leader Must Embrace* (Nashville, TN: HarperCollins Leadership, 2019).

7.  David Hunt, Sermon illustration, "Recognizing Opportunity."

8.  North Star to Freedom (U.S. National Park Service, n.d.), retrieved July 21, 2020, from https://www.nps.gov/articles/drinkinggourd.htm

## CHAPTER 5–GOOD THOUGHTS

1.  Dr. Seuss, *Oh, The Places You'll Go!* (New York, NY: Random House, 1990).

2.  Maria Millett, Michigan State University Extension, "Challenge Your Negative Thoughts," MSU Extension, October 2, 2018.

3.  Carlos Hathcock, quoted by Charles Henderson in Marine Sniper: The Explosive True Story of a Vietnam Hero (Briarcliff Manor, NY: Stein and Day Publishers, 1986).

4.  Peyton Sparks, Sermon illustration, "My Right Mind."

5.  Nick Saban and Brian Curtis, Foreword by Bill Belichick, *How good do you want to be? A champion's tips on how to lead and succeed* (New York, NY: Ballantine Books, 2017).

6.  Harvey Firestone, Brainy Quote

## CHAPTER 6–GOOD DECISIONS

1.  J. M. Barrie, *Peter Pan* (London, UK: Hodder & Stoughton, 1904).

2.  National Archives, n.d., "What If D-Day Failed? A Message from General Eisenhower," retrieved July 21, 2020, https://www.military.com/history/what-if-d-day-failed-message-from-general-eisenhower.html

## CHAPTER 8–ACTION–GET IT DONE

1.  Walt Mason, poem, "The Welcome Man."

2.  Amy Relich Cuddy, *Presence: Bringing Your Boldest Self to Your Biggest Challenges*, (New York, NY: Little, Brown and Company, 2015).

3.  R. Feloni, "How Alabama coach Nick Saban used psychology to build a football dynasty" (August 12, 2015), retrieved July 24, 2020,  https://www.businessinsider.com/alabama-coach-nick-saban-process-2015-8

4.  Stuart Diamond, *Getting More: How You Can Negotiate to Succeed in Work and Life* (New York, NY: Three Rivers Press, 2010), 371.

5.  "Don't Trust Feelings," sermoncentral.com, July 31, 2008.

## CHAPTER 9–WHEN REALITY STRIKES

1.  *Journals of the Lewis & Clark Expedition*, September 16, 1805, accessed September 15, 2020, https://lewisandclarkjournals.unl.edu/item/lc.jrn.1805-09-16.

## CHAPTER 10–LITTLE THINGS, BIG THINGS

1.  Dale Carnegie, *How to Win Friends and Influence People* (New York, NY: McGraw-Hill, 1968).

## CHAPTER 11–EMBRACE BIG MOMENTS

1.  Amy Cuddy, *Presence: Bringing Your Boldest Self to Your Biggest Challenges* (New York, NY: Little, Brown and Company, 2015), 267–8.

2.  Japanese Folklore, "House of 1000 Mirrors," https://www.great-inspirational-quotes.com/the-house-of-1000-mirrors.html

3.  Max Lucado, *Every Day Deserves a Chance: Wake up to the gift of 24 little hours* (Nashville, TN: Thomas Nelson, 2007).

4.  Anna Winthrop, "How to Start a Fashion Brand," Masterclass Online.

## CHAPTER 12–BUTTER ON TODAY

1.   James C. Hunter, *The World's Most Powerful Leadership Principle: How to become a servant leader* (New York, NY: Crown Business, 2004).
2.   Stump, S. (2019, December 04). "'Butter Man' explains how he's spreading joy after 'feud' with Al at parade," retrieved July 24, 2020, https://www.today.com/popculture/butter-man-how-he-s-spreading-joy-after-feud-al-t169150.
3.   L. Haefeli, "Priest's role as 'butter' in Thanksgiving Parade becomes a hit, spreads all over social media (December 4, 2019), retrieved July 24, 2020, from http://westchester.news12.com/story/41408294/priests-role-as-butter-in-thanksgiving-parade-becomes-a-hit-spreads-all-over-social-media

## CHAPTER 13–BUILDING UPON LAID FOUNDATIONS

1.   J. Wadler, "Calvin Klein's Partner Defines a Long Shot" (April 21, 1999), retrieved July 24, 2020, https://www.nytimes.com/1999/04/21/nyregion/public-lives-calvin-klein-s-partner-defines-a-long-shot.html
2.   Malcolm Gladwell, *The Tipping Point: How Little Things Can Make a Big Difference* (New York, NY: Little, Brown & Company, 2000, 2002).
3.   "Harrowing Tale of Scenes on Titanic by Miss Dowdell," *Encyclopedia Titanica*, 3 Sept. 2020, www.encyclopedia-titanica.org/harrowing-tale-scenes-titanic-miss-dowdell.html.
4.   *Ibid.*
5.   *Brené Brown on Empathy*, 2013, https://youtu.be/1Evwgu369Jw.
6.   *Ibid.*
7.   Jennifer Latson, "The Most Popular Game in History Almost Didn't Pass Go," (November 5, 2014), retrieved July 24, 2020, https://time.com/3546303/monopoly-1935/

## CHAPTER 14–HOT POTATO

1.   "Perseverance, Peace, and Purity (Hebrews 12:12–14)," Lesson 47, Bible.org., accessed September 17, 2020, https://bible.org/seriespage/lesson-47-perseverance-peace-and-purity-hebrews-1212-14.
2.   Founders Online: "From George Washington to Lewis Nicola," 22 May 1782 (n.d.), retrieved July 24, 2020, https://founders.archives.gov/documents/Washington/99-01-02-08501
3.   "*Godspeed* (Ship)." Wikipedia. Wikimedia Foundation, March 24, 2020. https://en.wikipedia.org/wiki/Godspeed_(ship).